TELEMARKETING: APPLICATIONS AND OPPORTUNITIES

Lloyd C. Finch
Vivyan A. Finch

A FIFTY-MINUTE™ SERIES BOOK

CRISP PUBLICATIONS, INC.
Menlo Park, California

TELEMARKETING: APPLICATIONS AND OPPORTUNITES

Lloyd C. Finch
Vivyan A. Finch

CREDITS
Managing Editor: **Kathleen Barcos**
Editor: **Janis Paris**
Typesetting: **ExecuStaff**
Cover Design: **Carol Harris**
Artwork: **Ralph Mapson**

Copyright © 1995 by Crisp Publications, Inc.

Printed in the United States of America by Bawden Printing Company.

English language Crisp books are distributed worldwide. Our major international distributors include:

CANADA: Reid Publishing Ltd., Box 69559—109 Thomas St., Oakville, Ontario, Canada L6J 7R4. TEL: (905) 842-4428, FAX: (905) 842-9327

Raincoast Books Distribution Ltd., 112 East 3rd Avenue, Vancouver, British Columbia, Canada V5T 1C8. TEL: (604) 873-6581, FAX: (604) 874-2711

AUSTRALIA: Career Builders, P.O. Box 1051, Springwood, Brisbane, Queensland, Australia 4127. TEL: 841-1061, FAX: 841-1580

NEW ZEALAND: Career Builders, P.O. Box 571, Manurewa, Auckland, New Zealand. TEL: 266-5276, FAX: 266-4152

JAPAN: Phoenix Associates Co., Mizuho Bldg. 2-12-2, Kami Osaki, Shinagawa-Ku, Tokyo 141, Japan. TEL: 3-443-7231, FAX: 3-443-7640

Selected Crisp titles are also available in other languages. Contact International Rights Manager Suzanne Kelly at (415) 323-6100 for more information.

Library of Congress Catalog Card Number 94-68577
Finch, Lloyd C. and Vivyan A.
Telemarketing: Applications and Opportunities
ISBN 1-56052-307-7

This book is printed on recyclable paper with soy ink.

ABOUT THIS BOOK

Telemarketing: Applications and Opportunities is not like most books. It has a unique "self-paced" format that encourages a reader to become personally involved. Designed to be "read with a pencil," there are exercises, activities, assessments and cases that invite participation.

The telemarketing approach suggested throughout this book will be one that offers a businesslike method of adding service and value to both in- and outbound customer calls.

This book will discuss telemarketing applications (both business-to-business and business-to-consumer), present the steps required to implement a successful program, and cover telemarketing techniques that are applicable to particular applications.

Telemarketing: Applications and Opportunities can be used effectively in a number of ways. Here are some possibilities:

—**Individual Study.** Because the book is self-instructional, all that is needed is a quiet place, some time and a pencil. Completing the activities and exercises will provide valuable feedback, as well as practical ideas for improving your business and enhancing your customer service.

—**Workshops and Seminars.** This book is ideal for use during, or as preassigned reading prior to, a workshop or seminar. With the basics in hand, the quality of participation will improve. More time can be spent practicing concept extensions and applications during the program.

—**College Programs**. Thanks to the format, brevity and low cost, this book is ideal for short courses and extension programs.

There are other possibilities that depend on the objectives of the user. One thing is certain: even after it has been read, this book will serve as excellent reference material that can be easily reviewed.

ABOUT THE AUTHORS

Lloyd and Vivyan Finch are the principles of Alpha Consulting Group, an organization that creates books and video training programs on subjects including telephone skills, teamwork, customer service and telemarketing. Lloyd and Vivyan founded the organization in 1984 after leaving their careers at Pacific Bell and AT&T. Vivyan worked extensively in Phone Power sales while with Pacific Bell and created numerous successful telemarketing programs. Lloyd has established profitable telemarketing programs for a variety of clients in the software and office products industries. Lloyd is the author of two other books by Crisp Publications, *Telephone Courtesy and Customer Service* and *Twenty Ways to Improve Customer Service.*

PREFACE

Telemarketing—an industry that produces $435 billion in annual revenues—is more than selling by telephone. Each incoming and outgoing customer call provides opportunities not only for telemarketing, but for improved customer service as well. To maximize these opportunities, a well-thought out program must first be developed and then successfully implemented.

Telemarketing takes an in-depth look at the opportunities that exist in almost every organization. This book identifies and describes numberous applications and discusses the skills and techniques required to turn these applications into profitable telemarketing programs. Emphasis is placed on planning in order to avoid the common problems and risks of most telemarketing programs.

Examples and case histories are presented, as well as valuable insight as to how telemarketing meets customer needs. The reader will learn a step-by-step approach to planning a successful telemarketing program, while keeping in focus enhancing customer satisfaction.

Lloyd C. Finch   Vivyan A. Finch

ACKNOWLEDGMENT

Special thanks to LifeScan Inc., Milpitas, California, for their generosity and willingness to share their customer service success story.

CONTENTS

SECTION

I

Telemarketing Basics

THE TELEMARKETING IMAGE

Telemarketing is often thought of as a "hard sell" method of marketing and as a result is dismissed. Many customer service operations employ telemarketing and people are concerned about mixing sales with customer service. Our perception of telemarketing is often a situation in which the customer requests service and the representative tries to sell something. The customer becomes irritated and finds someone else to handle his or her business.

Telemarketing: The Old Approach

Originally telemarketing applications were sell-by-telephone programs. The inexpensive telephone sale versus the expensive cost of a face-to-face customer visit was appealing; however, telemarketing (also called inside sales) groups often conflicted with outside sales. With outside sales controlling the operation, telemarketing groups typically handled incoming telephone orders—often thought of as a sales support function—and were allowed to handle only low-end product sales.

This thinking has not changed much today. Telemarketing is frequently an afterthought and not a planned part of the marketing mix. There are two basic reasons:

1. Management fails to support telemarketing, and

2. There is a lack of knowledge of telemarketing.

Telemarketing: The New Approach

Typically customer calls are managed without an attempt to upgrade the order. Although an order upgrade effort should not be made on every customer order, in most order-processing organizations opportunities can be found to upgrade at least a few orders. Does this mean a hard sell approach? No. It merely suggests that a telemarketing program might be developed around the process of a customer placing an order. Perhaps the program could consist of suggesting an alternative or addition to customers who order certain products or services. The alternative is offered as added information and service for the customer. Here are two examples.

THE TELEMARKETING IMAGE (continued)

How About Buying the Deluxe Model?

Suppose the customer places an order for a small pet carrier. The representative asks, "Did you consider our deluxe model?" If the customer says "yes"—that is the end of the telemarketing effort. If the customer response is "no," then an opportunity exists to briefly discuss the benefits of the fancier carrier with the customer. Suppose the difference in gross profit between the small and large pet carrier is $12. For every upgraded order an additional $12 in gross profit will be recorded. Multiply the increase by the number of upgraded orders and a significant figure might develop.

CASE STUDY: José Places an Order

José is a purchasing agent for a large organization. He calls one of his suppliers and places an order for stationery supplies. Janine handles the request and before she totals the order asks: "Do you need any computer paper today?" José replies, "I didn't know you carried computer paper. I was going to call another supplier with a paper order. What's your price?" Janine quotes her price and following a short discussion adds computer paper to the order.

Is it worth asking the customer a simple question? Is asking the customer one question over the phone really a telemarketing program? The answer to both questions is "yes."

TELEMARKETING: BUSINESS-TO-CONSUMER

Many of us think of telemarketing as that annoying phone call in the middle of our dinner. The caller quickly introduces him- or herself and then launches some sort of pitch for a product or service. Frequently there is little correlation between the call and our needs. Perhaps we live in a particular zip code and that translates into certain meaningful demographic information for the telemarketer.

The telemarketer may know our approximate income, years of education, whether we own or rent, and a wide assortment of other personal facts and figures. Based on this knowledge an assumption is made that we are prospects for her service or product.

The success of this style of telemarketing relies heavily on the number of calls. Few sales, often less than 1 percent, are made from a very high volume of calls.

Most of us find these business-to-consumer telemarketing calls annoying unless there is a match between our needs and the telemarketer's product or service.

> ## CASE STUDY: *Using Telemarketing Systematically*
>
> Marty owns Marty's Chimney Cleaning. In Marty's marketing area 90 percent of the homes have fireplaces. Two evenings a week Marty makes cold calls. He introduces himself and explains that he is a chimney sweep with over 10 years experience and asks if the homeowner is interested in having his chimney cleaned. Approximately 60 percent of all calls result in a short discussion about the homeowner's chimney, how much it is used and how often it should be cleaned. If the homeowner doesn't hire him immediately, Marty suggests he call back in six months or a year, whatever the homeowner feels is appropriate, and offer his services again. Marty reports the majority agree to the call back. Marty maintains a file on each homeowner who expresses interest in his services and records pertinent information such as type of chimney, number of fireplaces, the date of the last cleaning, and of course when to call back. Marty has a successful small business based on his work cleaning chimneys and his ability to execute telemarketing two nights a week.

TELEMARKETING:
BUSINESS-TO-CONSUMER (continued)

If you lived in Marty's area and had a fireplace in your home, would you mind a call, once a year, from Marty?

When there is a match between the customer's need and the service offered, the customer is not as bothered by the telemarketing call. When the match is marginal or nonexistent, the call can be seen as an invasion of privacy.

THE TELEMARKETER-CUSTOMER RELATIONSHIP

The relationship between a telemarketer and a prospect is key to the success of the call.

Telemarketing generates $435 billion and much of that revenue comes from a proactive outbound call to a customer or consumer. The telemarketer calls, establishes some rapport, engages the prospect in conversation, presents a product or service, and—when appropriate—tries to close the sale.

Let's look at one important aspect of the sales call: the relationship between telemarketer and prospect.

The Relationship

Sales center managers and telemarketers strive for volume and quality. Volume is a necessity because the average sales call fails. Quality is required to increase the probability of closing a sale. The stronger the relationship between the customer and prospect, the greater probability of a sale. Here's an illustration.

EXAMPLE: ABC Publications

Let's assume you ordered this book two weeks ago. The publisher, ABC Publications, waits two weeks and figures by then you have at least started reading the book and have perhaps finished it. A telemarketer calls and asks how you liked the book. The two of you have an interesting conversation regarding the merits of the book. During the course of the conversation the telemarketer asks what kind of work you do. You explain that you work in customer service and are also helping develop a new telephone skills training class for your organization. The telemarketer opens a discussion about another ABC book entitled, Terrific Telephone Techniques *and suggests it will fit well with your training plans. You agree and order one copy to preview. One week later the telemarketer calls again and asks how you liked the telephone skills book. You order 100 copies for your students.*

THE TELEMARKETER-CUSTOMER RELATIONSHIP (continued)

Why the Sale Was Made

The sale was possible because a relationship between the reader and the publisher existed. This relationship was enhanced when the telemarketer recognized another need. As the customer you probably do not feel a telemarketer called you to just sell more books. You probably feel the telemarketer also wanted to know your thoughts on the book you purchased.

When a relationship between prospect and telemarketer doesn't exist there is little point in the telemarketer making the call. There are only two reasons such a call might be made. First, the telemarketer is working the volume theory that says, make enough calls and eventually someone will buy. Or secondly, the telemarketer doesn't know any better.

In our example, you were already a customer of ABC Publications because a previous book had been purchased. Suppose that connection didn't exist. Why would the telemarketer call you?

Let's assume your name appears on a list of customer service supervisors that ABC purchased. How does that connect you to ABC? Let's look at it from the telemarketer's perspective. The telemarketer sees you as:

- Someone who needs customer service information

- Someone who probably is in a position to buy, make decisions, or at least recommend books

- As a prospect who reads about customer service

There is still a connection between what the telemarketer offers and your possible needs. Obviously, the relationship is not nearly as strong. Because of this, the customer's reaction to the call will be different and the telemarketer may have to be more persuasive to get the customer interested in books.

Why Is This Important?

The idea of a relationship is fundamental to the success of any telephone sales program. If, in your organization, you need new customers and are convinced telemarketing will help you, then find a reason to call the prospective customer. In the telemarketer's opening remarks, the reasons are explained to the prospect. This is done even on the so-called cold call. In fact, finding the right connection can quickly warm up the call. For example:

> *"Mr. Riley, I read in the paper that you are planning a 15,000-foot addition to your warehouse facilities. We provide air conditioning systems for many large buildings like yours and I thought . . ."*

The connection is the warehouse expansion and the need for air conditioning. Or:

> *"Megan, I know the bank uses considerable stationery supplies and we maintain a very large inventory. This means we can provide fast and often same-day service since we are so close. Do you presently have one of our catalogs?"*

The connection is the bank's stationery needs, physical location—close to bank—and the need for fast service.

If these connections sound like benefits, be assured they are. The relationship itself is often the strongest benefit for the prospect, at least initially. Later the other benefits your product or service offers become apparent.

When the Connection Is Limited

Some telemarketers, especially in the business-to-consumer marketplace, rely on the vaguest connection. Because you live in a specific zip code or your name appears on a certain list, the telemarketer—working on the volume theory—assumes you are a good candidate for his or her services. He calls, introduces himself and starts talking about a particular product or asks questions about your needs. When the timing is right or the sales pitch is effective, the telemarketer captures a new client. It usually takes a large number of calls to secure one new client or customer and for this reason (amongst others) many new to telemarketing fail.

THE TELEMARKETER-CUSTOMER RELATIONSHIP (continued)

Dialing for the Connection

What these professionals are doing is dialing and looking for the connection. When telemarketers are successful, it means they have connected their services to the prospect's needs and established a relationship.

REGULATIONS AND CONTROLS

In a limited number of cases facts have been misrepresented and actual cases of telemarketing fraud have occurred. However, it's important to keep in mind, the overwhelming majority of business-to-consumer telemarketers are honest and legitimate businesspeople. Everyone who makes cold calls has to be aware that customer perception of telemarketers is not always positive. When calling customers and conducting business on the telephone the highest standards of ethical behavior must prevail.

Who Regulates Telemarketing?

The Federal Communications Commission (FCC), Federal Trade Commission (FTC), Federal, and State Attorneys General offices are involved in the regulation of telemarketing.

Telemarketing, business to consumer, has become regulated by all but a few states. The laws covering telemarketing are concerned with monitoring of calls, use of automatic-dialing machines, hours of calling, 900 numbers, consumer protection regarding order cancellation, and a great deal more. New legislation, which will produce added restrictions on the telemarketer, is increasing each year.

Telemarketing Code of Ethics

The American Telemarketing Association (ATA) has adopted a code of ethics for all telemarketers: "The code of ethics has been developed under the premise that professional, reputable programs have specific goals, achieved through closely supervised, high-quality performance with the public interest (business and consumer) in mind." The ATA strongly urges all members to operate in accordance with all laws, business codes, and regulations.

TELEMARKETING *IS* DIFFERENT

Customers are generally less trusting and not quite as comfortable with telephone discussions and negotiations over the telephone as they are in face-to-face situations. The more serious, personal, or complex the situation, the more skill required by the telemarketer to make the customer comfortable.

There is a certain intimacy in a face-to-face customer meeting that is difficult to achieve in a telephone encounter. When seated face to face we read each other's smiles, warmth of personality, body language, and hundreds of other signals that make communication possible. When seated face to face the customer reads you, and at the same time you are developing a perception of him. These benefits disappear when we replace the sit-down meeting with a telephone conversation. The customer no longer sees you and must depend on your words, your voice, what you say, and what he or she thinks you said.

Remember: The Customer Can't See You

Tim liked to joke with customers and most customers found him likable and trustworthy. One of Tim's favorite face-to-face routines was to joke about the length of the contract he asked customers to sign. "We made this extra long so you wouldn't read all the fine print," was his standard line. Next, he would smile and laugh to let the customer know he was kidding. The customers enjoyed the joke. Handling a customer inquiry on the telephone one day, Tim was discussing the services his organization offered. The customer asked about the contract and Tim used his standard joke about the length of the contract. The customer didn't laugh. Instead the customer became uncomfortable with Tim and the issue of trust entered her mind. The difference between a face-to-face and a telephone customer was made clear to Tim.

SUMMARY

A connection must exist before a sale is made. This connection between telemarketer and prospect either exists prior to the call or is developed during the call. When calling prospective customers it is essential to try and find the connection before the call or as soon as possible during the call. Telemarketing without a strong prospect connection depends on the volume side of the telemarketing formula and represents a lot of work for the return.

SECTION

II

A Ten-Step Telemarketing Program

PLANNING TELEMARKETING

In this section we will discuss the 10 critical planning steps in creating a telemarketing program. The implementation of these steps will greatly assist you in the functions of planning, organizing, staffing, directing, and controlling a winning telemarketing program.

TEN STEPS TO SUCCESS

STEP #1: Identify the Application

STEP #2: Decide How the Program Will Work

STEP #3: Examine the Impact on the Organization

STEP #4: Determine Staffing Requirements

STEP #5: Evaluate Personnel Training Needs

STEP #6: Outline the Operation Costs

STEP #7: Set Reasonable Objectives

STEP #8: Establish a Measurement System

STEP #9: Develop a Monitoring System

STEP #10: Devise a Market Test Plan

Telemarketing: Applications and Opportunities

STEP #1: Identify the Application

As mentioned earlier, telemarketing programs are centered around either the incoming or outgoing customer call. Let's begin by looking at the incoming call. Determine under what circumstances customers call your organization. Your response might look like the following.

Incoming Customer Calls

Place a checkmark in each box that applies to your situation. Customers call us to:

☐ **1.** Place orders

☐ **2.** Check status of orders

☐ **3.** Question invoices, bills, or statements

☐ **4.** Receive technical or product assistance

☐ **5.** Schedule installations or repairs

☐ **6.** Change account, billing, or other information

☐ **7.** Make service or sales appointments

☐ **8.** Sign up for seminars

☐ **9.** Request catalogs or other brochures/information

☐ **10.** Make other inquiries

☐ Other _____

By closely examining incoming customer calls, a telemarketing opportunity will probably be found. The most common opportunity generally falls under customer inquiries. When customers call and ask about products or services, the timing is excellent for a telemarketing effort. The second most potent opportunity would be a customer placing an order. However, other customer incoming calls may be just as lucrative.

Outgoing Customer Calls

In looking for telemarketing opportunities there are two types of outgoing customer calls to consider. The existing outbound call and an outbound call that you would like to make:

1. Existing outbound calls such as scheduling service appointments and an assortment of customer follow-up calls may provide a telemarketing opportunity.

2. Outbound calls you would like to see made may include cold calls to new prospects, calls to existing customers, calls to inactive customers, and other customer calls.

A place to start with outbound calling is with a wish list. Suppose, for example, you wanted to contact all existing customers in a particular geographical area who purchased less than $5,000 in product or services in the last year. With this goal in mind, or one similar to it, design a telemarketing program with the intent of increasing the amount of business these customers do with your organization.

STEP #2: Decide How the Program Will Work

The strength of the application can be determined by visualizing how the program might work. Several people brainstorming the idea can produce some interesting results.

EXERCISE: My Work Flow Chart

Develop a work flow chart that begins with the customer call and leads to the telemarketing effort. Include names of employees who will conduct the telemarketing and managers who can supervise it. Be concerned about the level of quality you can put into the program (in terms of employees who will conduct the telemarketing and managers who can supervise the operation). Start thinking about realistic potential results. Develop some tentative operation costs.

Work Flow

Any planning beyond the initial discussion stage should include front-line employees who currently interface with customers and who will carry the responsibility for the new telemarketing effort. Their insight is invaluable.

Above all else consider the impact upon the customer:

- How will the customer react?

- Will the response be completely positive?

- What are the risks?

STEP #3: Examine the Impact on the Organization

A common pitfall in telemarketing planning is failing to consider how the organization will be affected. A typical example follows:

Willow Bank Offers Free Checking

Willow Mountain Bank was small and had difficulty competing with the larger banks. In order to gain new customers, Willow decided to offer a promotional program for new customers only. The offer was two years of free checking. The bank organized a telemarketing program and employees made evening calls to the local community offering free checking.

The employee would call and introduce herself, describe the free checking offer and the personalized service benefits of doing business with the bank, and then ask if the customer was interested.

The calls were well received because Willow Mountain Bank had a good reputation and free checking was appealing. The initial results of the program were excellent. Within three weeks 1,200 new checking accounts had been established.

The problem came when the new accounts desk tried to process all the information. They were immediately swamped and there was considerable delay in establishing the new checking accounts. Temporary checks, for the new customers, were delayed because the account information had to be entered in the computer before the checks could be sent. The check printer, suddenly loaded with orders, had to stretch his delivery interval by a week and this added to the overall delay.

Many of the new customers immediately closed their old checking accounts and awaited their new checks and account information from Willow. When even the temporary checks didn't show up, these customers became irritated and called the bank to complain.

Meanwhile, the telemarketing effort continued and a few hundred more new checking account applications were dumped on the new accounts desk.

Unexpectedly, the local newspaper printed a short article about the free checking promotion in the business pages. This irritated a large number of existing checking account customers who called the bank and asked why they were not offered free checking.

Willow Bank decided to halt the free checking promotion and reconsider their position. Although they had gained many new customers, almost a third had returned to their former banks because of the delay experienced in establishing their accounts. Although it could not be quantified, several of the bank employees felt that considerable ill will had been created with the bank's existing checking account customers.

In this example the application was strong and the overall concept good. But, the impact upon the new accounts desk became a problem. When a telemarketing program is successful the impact will usually be felt somewhere within the organization. When new products or service are sold, inventory, invoice processing, installation, tech support, shipping, and other functions are affected. Measuring the impact of telemarketing is a matter of studying the influence on each department or work unit. To avoid surprises and possible setbacks, this influence has to be taken into account and managed.

STEP #4: Determine Staffing Requirements

Who will do the telemarketing is always an important question. If a customer call is inbound, an inquiry for example, can the person normally handling the call include telemarketing in a response? Does the person possess the necessary skills? How much training will be required? These and other questions need to be addressed and thoroughly explored.

A common mistake is to assume a nonsales/service employee can manage customer conversations on the telephone. More than one clerk, order processor, or receptionist has been expected to handle some form of telemarketing activity. It rarely works out. Most clerical and other nonsales/service employees don't have the necessary skills to complete a telemarketing assignment.

In Step #3 we considered the telemarketing impact upon the organization. Staffing can easily be impacted. Imagine a successful inbound telemarketing program that upgrades 20 percent of orders. Suddenly, customer calls are twice as long as usual. Instead of inbound customer calls getting immediate attention, they have to wait or be called back. To resolve the situation, new representatives may have to be added. That increases cost, which may offset the increased revenue from upgrading orders. Keep in mind, staffing can easily be affected by telemarketing.

Two Considerations

When planning a staff to conduct telemarketing, there are two primary considerations:

1. **Quantity.** Is the staff large enough to handle the telemarketing program?

2. **Quality.** Are existing staff skills strong enough to put forth a quality effort?

The Quantity Issue

Obviously the staff must be large enough to manage the telemarketing task. If the objective, for example, is to establish an outbound customer calling program that will reach 5,000 existing customers in the next 30 days and tell them about your exciting new product, a large staff may be required. How large? Suppose your market test results in the average telemarketer completing eight calls an hour. Completing a call means actually talking to the customer. If the customer is interested, you learn that the call lasts 15 minutes; if not, it lasts two minutes but the average comes out to 7.5 minutes. With this average, you can closely approximate the number of telemarketers required to meet the objective. Use the following formula:

> The goal is 49 calls per day per telemarketer. The 30-day objective is to call 5,000 customers requiring 167 calls a day. 167 divided by 49 calls = 3.4 telemarketers needed. Of course, the math is easy but there are still unknowns. For example, will the telemarketers be able to maintain the pace required? Will administrative and follow-up tasks slow their progress? The program will have to be monitored on a continual basis if the objective is to be met.

The Inbound Quantity Issue

Planning the quantity side of an inbound telemarketing program is much different. Here the prospective customer is calling you and this poses several key questions. For example, how many of these customers can you afford to irritate because of telephone busy signals or slow responses? Can you afford to staff the program so that every customer gets an immediate answer? Most organizations can't. How will the customers react to waiting? Estimating the number of calls to be managed can be a complex task. More than one organization has staffed a telemarketing center in anticipation of a large number of calls resulting from national advertising or other promotion—only to receive minimal calls.

Large inbound telemarketing programs definitely require a market test. This may be a good place to consider contracting with an agency or hiring temporary telemarketers discussed under "Telemarketing Agencies" later in this section. The market test will provide a good idea of the number of calls to expect.

STEP #4 (continued)

Plan for the Busy Hour

Inbound customer calls peak during what's normally called the busy hour, which varies from business to business. During this hour as much as 20 percent of all daily calls will be realized. One theory suggests planning adequate staff for the busy hour, which will enable you to manage all other hours. However, that's an expensive way to do business. Ideally, staff is adjusted as much as possible for hours after the busiest hour, the second busiest hour, third busiest hour, and so on. If it is advertising that is driving the inbound customer call, most ad agencies have considerable expertise in planning for expected call volumes.

When the inbound call is a customer placing an order or making another inquiry, histories of calls are usually maintained. Having a history of inbound calls can prove invaluable in planning your staff.

Knowing, for example, what to expect from different business situations is essential. How many calls will seasonal business generate? How about calls for promotions, sales, new product introductions, and other special offerings?

Whether the inbound program is large or small, its success will be based on the quality displayed in managing the call, more so than the number of calls. One final point. Keep in mind that customers want fast service. Continual delays waiting to speak to a representative or numerous telephone busy signals will turn customers away.

The Importance of Planning

A staff who successfully manage a large number of inbound customer calls may be unable to do the same with an outbound call.

Why? _____

_____

What do you think the cause of the problem might be? _____

_____

What key assumption might be made in the telemarketing planning that may later prove to be incorrect? _____

_____

THE QUALITY ISSUE

THE DILEMMA: Asking a customer service employee to move from managing incoming calls to a proactive position of calling customers is a major step. The two calls are unalike and require different skills. During the inbound call the customer sets the tone by typically making a request. On the outbound call, a representative must take the initiative and find a way to get the customer interested and involved.

A SOLUTION: When telemarketing skills are not available in-house, consider the following:

1. Telemarketing agencies

2. Temporary Employees

Telemarketing Agencies

Using outside telemarketing agencies to conduct a telemarketing program is common. The telemarketing agency typically provides a full range of services, including 800-numbers, order taking, customer information gathering, and a host of other activities associated with telemarketing. These agencies are usually in a position to manage in- and outbound calls for both business-to-consumer and business-to-business calls. Depending upon their size, they may provide full services such as program planning, scripting, tracking, and analysis. Many offer telemarketing consulting services as well.

Telemarketing magazine, in an article about agencies, states: "Your selection of a telemarketing agency is no less important than adding any key personnel to your sales and marketing team." The article also adds: "The agency should be a strategic partner in your overall marketing mix and should possess a wealth of telemarketing skills and knowledge about your specific type of business."

As you would expect, the costs for a telemarketing contractor can vary greatly depending upon the service provided and region where it is offered. Check your local yellow pages for a listing of agencies.

Temporary Employees

Temporary employees are another alternative. The basic idea is to execute telemarketing with on-site temporary personnel who can be supervised as regular employees. Hourly temporary employees can be hired who have good telemarketing/customer skills and meet the organization's usual employment requirements. These temporary workers generally come from an agency, but former or retired employees can also be a source. Temporary workers who have sales, service, or other customer contact experience are often good candidates. Testing a telemarketing plan may be a good place to use temporary personnel.

STEP #5: Evaluate Personnel Training Needs

Let's begin this discussion with a strong affirmative statement. The statement is: Training is needed and required. When employees are expected to display certain telemarketing skills, they should have training in those skills. Even in situations in which the employee experience level is high, a review of skills and expectations is normally in order. Without at least minimal training, even the most basic telemarketing program will usually produce a poor result.

CASE STUDY: Super Systems

Super Systems produces and sells software. The marketing group decided they needed to increase overall customer knowledge in order to plan new advertising and other promotions. Marketing developed Phase I of the plan, which called for customer service and sales to ask each inbound customer three questions. The questions were:

1. How many computers do you have in your organization?

2. How many domestic and international locations does your organization have?

3. What is the size of your MIS staff?

Marketing met with sales and service management and presented the plan. During the discussion one of the sales managers asked about training. The response from marketing was: "Why do we need training to get three questions answered?" The sales manager explained the need for training in order to implement the plan and to insure uniform results. He said, "These three questions, according to the plan, will be asked of several thousand customers over a six-week period of time by 40 sales or service reps. We want our reps asking the identical questions, recording the responses in the same manner, providing exact explanations as to our purpose for asking these questions, and responding in a similar manner when a customer asks questions or refuses to answer. In addition," he continued, "we want the reps to do their regular job and not let this survey interfere. To do that they need training."

EXERCISE: What's Your Reaction?

1. Why do you think the sales manager is right or wrong? _____

   _____

2. What, if any, training is required to insure the accuracy and success of the survey? _____

   _____

REVIEW

Just as marketing initially did at Super Systems, training is sometimes overlooked in telemarketing planning. Part of the reason is our perception of training as a very involved process. To get the three questions asked, a formal off-site two-day training class is not required. Perhaps a brown bag session will suffice. Input from the reps who will be asking the three questions is also important. In our example, experienced and highly skilled reps will need little more than general direction. Others will require instruction on how to work the three questions into the conversation. The bottom line is: training is usually a must and is always a consideration in the planning process.

STEP #6: Outline the Operation Costs

Once operation costs are established, the expected result can be measured against it and a decision as to the value of the telemarketing program can be made.

Often forgotten are the so-called hidden costs—costs such as mail that precedes or follows the telemarketing effort. Brochures and catalog costs can also add up quickly. Time is another possible hidden cost. Total transaction time to complete a telemarketing call may be much longer than thought when preparation, conversation, and follow-up are considered. Support services also come into play and should be considered. Other possible cost areas are as follows:

- Awards/Contests
- Compensation
- Computer Training
- Database Development
- Impact on Organization
- Incentives
- Mail
- Management

- Personnel
- Printing
- Prospect Lists
- Shipping
- Software
- Supervision
- Telephone

STEP #7: Set Reasonable Objectives

Generally, two problems are encountered when trying to set objectives:

1. Making the objective realistic, and

2. Quantifying the expected result. Once an objective is quantified, it becomes much easier to manage and measure.

Obviously, if a program is a sales effort or similar to one, quantifying is straightforward. The XYZ method works well. X number of units/services, sold for Y amount of dollars within Z time frame is a standard approach. In a nonsales circumstance, quantifying the objective is less obvious.

In our Super Systems example, three questions were to be asked on the inbound customer call. A quantified objective might be to receive a three-question response from 90 percent of all customers who call. This objective can easily be measured by tracking the number of calls and the number of completed questions. Usually, some sort of meaningful quantified objective can be established.

Making the objective realistic is a real concern. If the objective is set too high, the telemarketers usually know it immediately. When they firmly believe it is too high, their effort will diminish. Conversely, when the objective is realistic and attainable, they are motivated to meet or exceed the goal. This is especially true if they participated in setting the objectives. Failure to include the telemarketer in this process is viewed as just another "tops-down" management decision.

Quantifying the objective also helps focus the employee's effort. When the employees know they are expected to get 90 percent completion on the three questions, they can strive for that objective and monitor their own progress.

GUIDELINES FOR SETTING OBJECTIVES

STEP # 7 (continued)

Guidelines for Setting Objectives

There are three guidelines to follow that will help set realistic telemarketing objectives:

1. **Don't confuse what is needed with an attainable objective.**

   For example, in order to meet the year-end sales goal, the management of Super Systems sets the fourth-quarter objective 20 percent higher than the previous quarters. The objective is unattainable without some sort of windfall sale, and, as a result, the salespeople are frustrated and their effort slows.

2. **Include the telemarketer in setting objectives.**

3. **Be willing to alter and change the objective.**

Ideally, objectives should be flexible in both directions. If the telemarketing force easily meets the objective, then an increase is in order for the next quarter or next time period. When it is apparent the objective is unattainable, then a decrease is required.

STEP #8: Establish a Measurement System

A quality measurement system for telemarketing is similar to any other system an organization might use to measure sales, productivity, or other activities. There are four components:

1. **The Objective:** Measure actual results against the expectation.

2. **The Interval:** Measure with enough frequency to eliminate or greatly reduce the chance of failure and to determine when action is required.

3. **The Activities:** Measure the success and timing of employee activities that support the desired result. Alter and introduce new activities as required.

4. **Sharing the Results:** Let the telemarketers know their status by sharing the measurement-system findings. Ask for their input and ideas on how to improve the program and the measurement system.

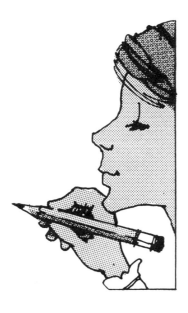

STEP #9: Develop a Monitoring System

Monitoring and measurement go somewhat hand in hand because they occur simultaneously. In the telemarketing plan the monitoring/controlling responsibility must be assigned. A supervisor, manager, individual, or telemarketing team carry the monitoring responsibility.

There is an old, but important, management principle that applies to the idea of monitoring and controlling. The principle says you can't control the results, but you can manage the activities that produce the results.

All activities in a quality telemarketing effort can be planned, monitored, and controlled. As an example, at Super System Inc. the sales and service reps are trying to get 90 percent of inbound customers to answer three questions. To achieve this objective, several activities have to take place. Those activities include:

- Training development

- Actual training, perhaps a market test to validate the training procedures

- Monitoring of employee's performance

- Resolving individual employee problems

- Tracking results at frequent intervals

- Summarizing results for marketing

- Other activities as appropriate

DON'T FORGET TO DEVISE A MARKET TEST PLAN!

STEP #10: Devise a Market Test Plan

Before Super Systems Inc. launched their telemarketing program, a three-day market test was conducted. Several experienced reps asked the three questions of each customer they spoke with. The results of the test were as follows:

1. 70 customers were interviewed

2. 60 (85 percent) responded to all three questions

3. 6 customers said they didn't have time

4. 4 didn't want to answer the questions

5. Telemarketers reported customers were generally cooperative.

6. The survey answers received posed new questions.

7. Since experienced reps could only get 85 percent of customers to respond, it was thought that less experienced reps would get around 70 percent. It was agreed the 90 percent objective was too high.

8. Marketing began discussing a possible mail survey.

9. Sales management reported the test had provided insight as to how training should be developed and conducted.

10. Everyone was pleased that a test had been conducted before launching the entire program.

The Super Systems test proved to be worthwhile and illustrates the importance of the market test concept. Once the results of the test were known, the telemarketing program looked different to everyone involved.

EXERCISE: Program Review

Think about a telemarketing program you have knowledge of. Is it successful?

1. Do you think the planning steps discussed were used? _____

    _____

    _____

2. If they weren't, do you think the program would be more successful
    if the steps were utilized? _____

    _____

    _____

3. If you have been involved in a telemarketing effort, revisit the situa-
    tion and apply the planning steps. When the review is complete,
    determine if using the planning steps would change how the program
    was conducted. _____

    _____

    _____

SUMMARY

The steps work and need to be utilized regardless of the complexity of the
telemarketing program. Skipping or dismissing one step in the planning
process can negatively impact the telemarketing effort. Employing these steps
will improve the probability of a successful telemarketing program.

SECTION

III

The Telemarketing Application: Learning By Example

THE IMPORTANCE OF THE TELEMARKETING APPLICATION

A basic premise of telemarketing—Step 1 of the ten-step program—is the stronger the application the greater the probability the program will be successful. Makes sense, doesn't it? Surprisingly, telemarketing programs are often attempted based on weak applications. Keep in mind that no amount of planning or execution will overcome a poor or marginal application.

Let's look at a case where the application is . . . well, you decide. Is it strong, marginal, or weak?

CASE STUDY: Call the Guest Program

In the hospitality industry (hotel/motel) it is common for many hotels or resorts to maintain a mailing list of frequent guests. Periodically information about activities or special rates are mailed to former guests. The mailings are primarily designed to keep the organization's name in front of the guest. However, most report an immediate increase in reservation activity following the mailings.

The Ranch Lodge and Resort decided to suspend their mailing and instead place telephone calls to the guests. The plan called for contacting all 2,800 guests on the mailing list.

Two reservation clerks were to make telephone calls for three hours each evening until all guests had been contacted. The objective was for each clerk to complete 30 calls per night.

The reservation manager spent time training the clerks on what to say and how to respond to the guests. A short, to-the-point telemarketing message was developed. Guest questions were anticipated and the appropriate answers were rehearsed and mentally scripted.

The telemarketing message began with an introduction followed by a "thank you" for previous visits. Next, the reservation clerk told the guest about the special discount rate for former guests and then asked if she could book a reservation.

Following two weeks of calling, the results were as follows:

744 attempted calls

446 completed calls (talked with the guest)

357 calls where the entire message was delivered

260 no answers, left message, or not available

 38 wrong numbers or no longer in service

  3 guest reservations, total value $1,500.00

overtime cost for reservation clerks $590.00

telephone expense $475.00
_____
NET INCOME $435.00

It was also reported that as many as 20 guests said they were planning on making reservations in the near future.

A postcard mailing to 2,800 guests normally costs about $1,000.

EXERCISE: *What Do You Think?*

In judging the success of the program, there are several key questions to be answered. Answers to these questions will provide valuable insight into the "Call the Guest" program. A few of the questions call for speculation on your part. Using your best judgment, come up with an answer.

1. Do you think this is a good application for telemarketing? Why? _____
   _____

2. Are the results worth the effort and expense? _____
   _____

3. Would you continue with the program? Why or why not? _____
   _____

4. How do you think the program compares with the normal mail approach? _____
   _____

5. Even though the results aren't very good, do you think some good-will is being created? Will future reservations be made because of the telemarketing? _____
   _____

6. Twenty guests said they plan on making reservations in the near future. Do you think the telemarketing call influenced their decision?
   _____
   _____

One Perspective

This case illustrates the difficulty of telemarketing planning and execution in the absence of a strong application. There is no evidence to indicate the "Call the Guest" program is as effective as the direct-mail program. The mail program reaches everyone, whereas the telemarketing program has failed to reach nearly 40 percent of the guests on the first try. Of course, this is not to say that all the mail gets opened and read. By the time telemarketing reaches all guests on the mailing list, the projected costs of this program will be quite high. Based on the early reservation results, the program costs may not be justified.

THE IMPORTANCE OF THE TELEMARKETING APPLICATION (continued)

Calls to Recorders and Voice Mail Adds Cost

When planning telemarketing of this type, it's important to keep in mind the high rate of call completion due to recorders and voice message systems. The telephone and long distance companies love it, but when 20 percent of all calls in an evening are completed to a recorder or voice message system, it can get expensive. The large organization or frequent telemarketer can substantially reduce the costs by purchasing special-rate lines such as WATS (Wide Area Telephone Service) or using equipment that senses a machine answer and immediately disconnects; but, for a program conducted once or twice a year like "Call the Guest," the costs can add up.

Let's conclude the discussion regarding the "Call the Guest" program with these thoughts.

- The program had limited success.

- The projected costs are high considering the probable return.

- It is doubtful this telemarketing effort will be more worthwile than the direct mail plan.

Does this mean other "Call the Guest" programs won't work? No. Every situation is different and the results might be just the opposite in another environment. In the next section we will discuss how to plan and implement a successful telemarketing program.

TELEMARKETING SUCCESSES

Telemarketing success is not easy to come by. It takes a strong application, planning, execution, skill, and at times a great deal of patience and persistence. However, the rewards of organizing and implementing a successful program can be great.

The following two case studies are illustrations of telemarketing successes. Each case represents a different telemarketing application and industry. As you read these case studies, look for what is common to each situation and what makes the telemarketing program successful.

CASE STUDY: Smith Bottling Company

Smith Company is a small manufacturer and distributor of plastic bottles. Their customers are bottlers of cleaning chemicals, food processors, juice, and other businesses who have bottling requirements. Nearly 80 percent of their customers are located within a 200-mile marketing area. Smith provides a high service level to their market area by offering competitive pricing and fast delivery. Smith personally provides truck delivery to their accounts.

Smith customers have learned they don't need to carry a large inventory of bottles because they can place "just in time" orders and receive fast delivery. This procedure saves the customer the cost of maintaining a large inventory. Because of the high number of small orders, Smith knows the "just in time" approach is a more expensive method of doing business. The system, however, has helped lock in their customers. Other bottle manufacturers and distributors are unwilling to provide the service Smith does for small orders.

TELEMARKETING SUCCESSES (continued)

The Problem

Delivery costs were a major expense at Smith and increasing at the rate of 15 percent per year. Smith management became increasingly concerned about these costs and the negative impact they had on profits. Other carriers were considered as an alternative, but it was felt flexibility and personal service would be diminished if they discontinued personal delivery. The fact the delivery trucks were carrying only partial loads was adding greatly to costs. It was common, as an example, for a truck to leave only 25 percent full. Smith seriously considered establishing larger minimum orders and also stretching the delivery intervals so a truck could begin a route carrying a larger load. Sales argued this would diminish their high service level, perhaps offend long-standing customers, and eventually result in lost business.

The Telemarketing Plan

Following considerable discussion, Smith hit upon an important idea. They decided to try to increase their delivery truck load by using telemarketing. The following telemarketing plan was developed.

1. In an attempt to increase the truck load, accounts along the route would be called and asked if they have an order.

2. One outside salesperson would move inside part-time to make customer calls. Shipping would advise sales of the truck route two days in advance. Sales would initially call the large accounts along the truck route and ask if they have orders to place. If there was still truck capacity, smaller accounts along the route would be called. Sales would explain the program and purpose of the call to each account and maintain an order history so accounts wouldn't be called too often. Each account would also be offered the option of not being included in future calling.

3. The impact of a successful program meant the trucks would carry more orders per delivery route, thereby reducing delivery costs. Also, the order desk would have less work because the salesperson would be "intercepting" customer orders.

4. The sales and service manager agreed to develop and conduct one-on-one training with the salesperson making the calls.

5. The sales manager would be responsible for measuring, monitoring, and controlling the telemarketing program. A measurement system would be established that would track:

- Number of customer calls

- Gross sales

- Average value per sale

- Large account sales versus smaller account sales

- Telephone costs

- Decrease in order-desk customer calls

- Increase in delivery truck load size

6. An initial objective of increased load volume of 20 percent per truck was agreed to.

7. A two-week market test was planned.

Results

The telemarketing program went smoothly from the first day. The salesperson was able to call accounts along the truck route and intercept a few orders. Several of the customers liked the idea so much they requested a call anytime a delivery truck was coming into their area. Less than 2 percent of the customers objected to the idea and did not want to be called.

The two-week market test added 15 percent loading to the trucks. Over the next 60-day period the truck loading increased by nearly 25 percent. Delivery costs were cut by nearly 12 percent per order over this period.

The anticipated drop-off in customer calls at the order desk was greater than expected. It was decided that one of the order-desk employees would start working with the salesperson in order to eventually take over the job of calling customers along the truck route. This would allow the salesperson to return to her accounts fulltime.

TELEMARKETING SUCCESSES (continued)

> ## CASE STUDY: *Old Republic Paper Company*
>
> Old Republic Paper was successful and continuing to grow after nearly 35 years of operation. Outside salespeople called on their accounts face to face, providing service and generating sales. Customers called the order-processing group for routine or small orders in between sales visits. All accounts were assigned to a salesperson, which meant each salesperson had nearly 100 accounts. Of course, only the top 20 were considered active and required frequent face-to-face sales calls. The smaller accounts were usually called on once or twice during the year.

The Problem

Old Republic Paper knew that nearly 80 percent of their sales came from about 20 percent of their accounts. This was common within the paper industry. Management was concerned about this dependence on the larger accounts. Of equal concern was the growing competition from other paper suppliers who were placing more emphasis on the small accounts than Old Republic was.

A sales plan was organized requiring the salespeople to make more face-to-face calls on the smaller accounts. The salespeople didn't buy into the plan with much enthusiasm because they simply didn't have the time to call on many small accounts. Following a few months of the sales plan, small-account sales showed little increase.

The Telemarketing Plan

Sales management decided to take action. Following several weeks of meetings and discussion, they developed a small-account plan. Two employees from the order processing group were selected to form a new group called "inside sales." The purpose of the two-person group was to establish regular telephone sales contact with all small accounts. A two-month market test was agreed to. No objectives were established for the test period because no one knew what to expect. A sales manager was assigned to work with and train the inside sales employees. All sales would be credited to the outside sales person who had responsibility for the small account.

The market test results showed a 30 percent increase in sales volume from the small accounts. Based on the market test, a telemarketing plan was organized and implemented. The highlights of the plan were as follows:

1. Outside sales were asked to turn over all current accounts where annual billing was less than $10,000. Once inside sales developed a small account to $20,000 in annual billing, they were required to trade the account to outside sales. In return, outside sales traded in new small accounts they had established. Sales objectives and a compensation plan for inside sales was established.

2. Inside sales called all small accounts on a regular basis. Buying cycles and small-account paper inventory information was maintained by inside sales and used as a determining factor in generating future calls.

Results

In the first year, sales to small accounts increased by 40 percent. The inside sales people doubled their previous annual income. The inside sales people became very good with the timing of their calls to the small accounts. They called when the account's inventory was expected to be low. Much of the success was attributed to the special attention the small accounts felt they were getting from Old Republic Paper. The program was expanded to include branch locations of the paper company.

TELEMARKETING SUCCESSES (continued)

EXERCISE: Compare the Two Cases

The two cases you just read have several common links. For one thing, they were successful.

What else do they have in common? _____

_____

Think about the cases for a moment and then list five common factors that added to their success.

1. _____

2. _____

3. _____

4. _____

5. _____

SUMMARY

There are several correct answers when naming factors that added to the success of the cases.

- Foremost is the application itself. Each case had a strong telemarketing application.

- Planning should also be at the top of your list because each case was well thought out and planned.

- Execution of the plan.

- Training and assigning responsibility.

- Establishing objectives.

- Establishing a measuring and monitoring system.

- Conducting a market test before launching into the program.

SECTION

IV

Identify Telemarketing Opportunities

TELEMARKETING OPPORTUNITIES

In this section we will look at different telemarketing applications and the employee telephone skills required for each one.

OPPORTUNITY #1: Making Appointments

Appointments are made with customers and prospects by either the person who desires to meet with the customer or by another employee who is seeking the appointment for a co-worker. Both are strong telemarketing applications, with the latter being a real time-saver for the person who has the luxury of someone making his or her appointments.

The appointments may be made for the customer to come in or, more typically, meet at the customer's location. In either case the approach is to state the customer benefits of the appointment. In other words, what's in it for the customer? The customer, prospect, or client needs a good reason for the appointment. Let's discuss making appointments for others.

EXAMPLE: Susan Fills the Chair

Susan is the office administrator for Patricia, a dentist. To maximize the dentist's time and office income, Susan keeps the chair full by making and changing appointment times. Each week appointments are changed and cancelled by patients. When this happens, Susan calls other patients in an attempt to fill the void created by the changed appointment times. She knows the patients well and is familiar with most of their schedules. Her technique varies depending upon who she calls, but her requests are always stated in terms of benefits to the patient. Here are a few examples of the language and technique Susan uses.

"Mrs. Lau, I know you prefer early appointments and I have an opening on Thursday morning at eight. May I change your appointment from Friday afternoon?" [Benefit: the morning appointment.]

"Kim, you said you were anxious to get your dental work done. I can move your appointment up by two days. Is Monday morning at ten a good time for you?" [Benefit: getting the dental work done early.]

Susan might approach a long-term and very cooperative patient with: "Pete, I wonder if you can help the doctor. I need to move your appointment to Wednesday at three. Is that a good time for you?" [Benefit: patient gets to help the doctor.]

OPPORTUNITY #1 (continued)

Susan's telemarketing concept is similar to the bottling company we discussed earlier. The bottler was filling trucks and Susan is filling the doctor's chair. Think of all the telemarketing opportunities there are in trying to fill or complete something. For example, the customer's inventory, appointment calendars, schedules, use of cars and other vehicles, seminars, conferences, training sessions, membership rolls, donor lists, service appointments, volunteer lists, and many others. List three specific examples of such telemarketing opportunities that exist in your organization.

1. _____

   _____

2. _____

   _____

3. _____

   _____

Making Appointments for Others

In order to save the valuable time of salespeople, it is common for organizations to employ others to make sales appointments. The sales-support person calls the prospect or customer and sets an appointment for the salesperson to meet face to face with the client. In nonsales situations appointments are made for service, delivery, maintenance, and a host of other customer-serving functions.

There are two issues that nearly always surface in this type of telemarketing program:

► **ISSUE ONE: Coordinating Time Availability**

► **ISSUE TWO: Qualifying a Prospect**

ISSUE ONE: Coordinating Time Availability

When sales support gets a customer interested in an appointment, they should be able to set the time and date immediately. Sales support needs to have either a block of sales time set aside for appointments or control of the salesperson's calendar. Control over the calendar provides the most flexibility and allows sales support to close the appointment immediately.

ISSUE TWO: Qualifying a Prospect

The quality of the appointment is often an issue. The salesperson couldn't make the sale so he blames sales support for making a lousy appointment. Sales support argues the sale should have been made because the prospect was qualified. Some very serious finger-pointing can result. This issue by itself has ended many appointment-making telemarketing efforts. It must be addressed up front and continually dealt with. Cooperation and communication between sales and support are essential.

One solution is for sales to define a qualified appointment. In fact it is a must. Next, sales support should meet the criteria laid out by sales for qualifying and making appointments. Here's an example.

EXAMPLE: The Office Product Company

In an attempt to improve sales, an organization sets up a "making appointments" market test at their regional sales office. Two temporary telemarketers are hired and trained. Their task is to make sales appointments with prospects and existing customers for the salespeople. The motivation behind the program is to free up sales time. Sales management and telemarketing agree that all appointments must be qualified. To be qualified, sales management states that the following criteria must be met.

- *The prospect must be a decision maker with authority to buy.*

- *There must be a need for the product.*

- *The prospect must be interested in the product.*

- *The prospect or customer must have the money to buy.*

OPPORTUNITY #1 (continued)

The telemarketers make calls into various markets at the direction of sales. For the four-week market test period telemarketing manages the appointment calendars of the salespeople.

A high volume of calls are made in order to get a qualified appointment. Eight percent of all calls result in a qualified appointment. Remember that the appointment percentage is strongly influenced by the market called. Sales management decides to test two new markets where the application for their product is limited. The results from this experiment are poor, with a reduced overall percentage of appointments qualified.

CONSTRUCTING THE CONVERSATION

In order to qualify an appointment, telemarketers rely heavily on training and a script, prepared by an outside consultant. The script consists of benefit statements and questions. The customer response to the questions directs the flow of the conversation. For example, following the introduction the telemarketer might ask: "Are you familar with my office products company?" If the answer is "no," the telemarketer might briefly discuss the company in terms of products, size, and financial strength. Next, or if the answer to the previous question is "yes," the conversation moves to a discussion of particular office products the customer might be using. If the customer is using a competitor's product, discussion about how well it is functioning is attempted. If the customer isn't using a particular office product, there is a discussion as to "why not." When there appears to be a need for a product, it is briefly presented in order to stimulate interest. Again, strong benefit statements about the product are used along with questions designed to get the customer involved.

If the customer expresses interest with questions and positive comments, the telemarketer asks for the appointment. When the appointment is secured, the telemarketer further qualifies the appointment by asking questions about authority and money. A typical telemarketing conversation is provided for you here.

Typical Telemarketing Conversation

TELEMARKETER: "Good, the appointment is set for Wednesday at ten. Now I just have a couple of questions if you don't mind. I know this is premature, but if you should decide to purchase our office product, would you make that decision yourself or would others be involved?"

The customer's answer provides the telemarketer with information regarding the customer's level of involvement. The customer often says he or she would make the final purchasing decision. However, other employees and managers might participate and therefore influence the decision. The telemarketer should suggest or ask if these other individuals can be involved in the appointment.

CONSTRUCTING THE CONVERSATION (continued)

The final question asked of a prospect is about money.

TELEMARKETER: "In your financial planning for this year, did you budget for a new office product?"

When strong rapport is established or when the prospect is especially cooperative, follow-up questions concerning money are often asked. Examples might be:

TELEMARKETER: "How much did you budget? Since you have already included the office product in your budget, when are you planning on purchasing?"

In talking with organizations, telemarketers find that a new office product is sometimes not budgeted. When confronted with this situation, the telemarketer asks questions similar to what follows.

TELEMARKETER: "Since this year's budget doesn't include a new office product, will it be difficult for you to purchase one?"

SAMPLE SALES REFERRAL FORM

Qualified Appointment's Information

Telemarketing should record all qualified appointment information on a form and give it to sales. A sample form might look like this:

SALES REFERRAL

From: _____

Appointment time and date: _____

Customer name: _____

Telephone: _____ Customer org. name: _____

Address: _____ City: _____

Customer's decision-making position? _____
_____

What is the need for our office product? _____
_____

How did customer demonstrate interest in office product? _____
_____

Comments:_____
_____

Remember that those securing appointments usually have high expectations regarding those they qualify. Sales staff similarly have expectations of those setting appointments to ensure that prospects are highly qualified. Ideally, problems should be anticipated and discussed up front.

THE FIVE-STEP APPROACH TO MAKING APPOINTMENTS

The following techniques can be useful to all sales staff:

1. Introduce yourself and your organization.

- Build rapport when possible

2. State the purpose of the call using customer benefits.

- Continue building rapport
- Use references when appropriate

3. When appropriate, qualify the prospect

- identify objections and strive to overcome them.

4. Ask for the appointment stating customer benefits.

5. Close the conversation with a customer benefit statement.

The Service Call

The service manager at Jordan Auto Center closely monitors service appointments in order to help plan the work load for the mechanics. When he sees a slowing in the service schedule, he makes early evening telemarketing calls to customers who have cars due for service. Here is a sample conversation:

SERVICE MANAGER: "Good evening, Mrs. Lee. This is Phil from Jordan Auto Center. [Customer response.] I am calling to thank you for your business in the past and also because my records indicate your car is overdue for service. We last serviced it in March and in order to stay current with your warranty, we should have the car in soon. Did you see our advertisement featuring the $29.95 service special? [Waits for response.] Your savings with the special is ten dollars and that's good until the end of next week. I still have openings available—may I schedule an appointment for you?"

In this short telemarketing message there are three customer benefits. First, the reminder about maintaining the requirements of the warranty is very important to the customer. Second, the dollar savings. A third benefit is the call itself. The service manager calls to schedule an appointment; thus the customer doesn't have to be concerned about remembering to do so.

When Setting an Appointment Is Not Enough

The difficult call for most people is the so-called cold call to a prospective customer. In this call, the customer is presented with the benefits of the proposed meeting. The salesperson must sell the customer on the appointment and *at the same time* qualify the prospect.

A prominent businesswoman once said, "If the salesperson fails to qualify the prospect, then the only thing that usually gets sold is an appointment." The definition of a qualified appointment varies depending on the needs of the salesperson and the organization. In the office product case a qualified appointment might be a meeting with a decision maker who has a need for the product, is interested in purchasing, and has the money to purchase.

In other organizations, with different products or services, the criteria for qualification might be very different. For example, every salesperson wants to meet with decision makers, but that is not always possible. Often sales must meet with employees who influence decisions rather than make them— or with someone like a purchasing agent who just moves the product or service information to the next level.

Some salespeople are so confident, they believe they can sell most prospects if they can only secure an appointment. Others are so happy with an appointment they are afraid to attempt to qualify for fear they will lose the appointment. Sales behavior is interesting and sometimes bizarre.

A "QUALIFIED" SUCCESS

Frank is a successful real estate salesperson with ten years of experience. Frank says of his career: "I qualify every prospect and have become very successful." Frank says he qualifies most of his clients on the telephone during their initial conversation. He tries to determine how serious the potential buyer is, whether the individual is financially capable of buying a home, and asks about the buyer's time frame. Let's look at Frank's techniques for qualifying and making appointments:

FRANK: Good morning, Mr. Edwards, this is Frank Green with Fuller Realty. You called regarding the Maple Street house in Essex.

EDWARDS: Yes I did. We would like to take a look at it.

FRANK: Good. I'll be glad to show it to you.

At this point in the conversation many real-estate salespeople would simply set an appointment time. Wallace says this is what he used to do, but now he qualifies the prospect. He reports that the majority of the time it works. Let's listen in.

FRANK: What prompted your interest in the Maple Street house?

EDWARDS: We like the neighborhood and we need a bigger house.

FRANK: Where do you live now?

EDWARDS: We're in Middleton near the library.

FRANK: I'm familiar with that area. That's a nice neighborhood as well.

EDWARDS: Thanks. We have sort of outgrown the house. The schools aren't what they used to be either.

FRANK: How many children do you have?

EDWARDS: Three. Two girls and a boy.

FRANK: I'm sure you know the Essex School District is highly rated—one of the top five in the state.

EDWARDS: That's another reason we're thinking about moving.

FRANK: Are you planning on selling your existing house?

EDWARDS: Yes, we will have to sell it.

FRANK: The market is pretty strong in Middleton right now. I'll need your address so I can look up the comparables on your house. That will give us a good idea of what to ask for it. If you don't mind my asking, what's your equity position?

EDWARDS: We owe about $30,000.

FRANK: Well, that certainly puts you in a good position to buy in Essex. When would you like to see the house?

The conversation goes on for a few minutes and Frank sets the appointment and gets an agreement to look at a few other houses with Mr. Edwards and his wife.

COMBINING THE SKILLS

Cindy, like most salespeople, makes her own appointments. Most Mondays Cindy can be found in the office calling prospects and filling her appointment calendar. Selling office systems to the retail market is a demanding job. Using the techniques discussed earlier, Cindy is generally pretty successful in getting the appointments she wants. In the following example Cindy is calling Susan Davis, who is the controller at Powell's Department Store.

CINDY: "Good morning, Susan, my name is Cindy Long from Memory Systems. The reason for my call is I am a retail specialist with my company and work with stores like yours in setting up profitable office systems. Some of my customers you might know are Dale Fong at Abby's Store and Eileen Grafton at the Patio Center. Do you know either Dale or Eileen?"

SUSAN: "I know Dale well but I don't feel that we're interested in a new system at this point."

CINDY: "I recently worked closely with Dale and just completed a new system design and installation. Have you considered making a change?"

SUSAN: "Sure. But it's expensive and we have other priorities at this time. I wasn't aware Dale had made a change. What did they do?"

CINDY: "Dale gave me permission to mention the installation—our Vantage System. What system are you using?"

SUSAN: "Cash Systems."

CINDY: "The 1000 or their 2600?"

SUSAN: "I wish I could answer with the 2600, but it's the 1000 system."

CINDY: "How well is the 1000 working for you?"

SUSAN: "It's old and out of date, but it works."

CINDY: "How's the response time?"

SUSAN: "Well, that's a problem."

CINDY: "Response time was one of the big reasons Dale decided to make a change. He said they just couldn't live with delayed customer transactions any longer."

SUSAN: "That's the situation we're getting to."

At this point in the conversation Cindy has successfully introduced herself, engaged Susan in conversation, used an important reference, and uncovered the slow response time concern which will probably lead to a need for a new system. Cindy's next step is to further qualify the prospect and then ask for the appointment.

CINDY: "The customer transaction response time can be a real problem. Our new Vantage System eliminates the problem by dedicating a port for every point-of-sale terminal."

SUSAN: "That must be expensive."

CINDY: "Not really. Our pricing is competitive. Of course, there's a big savings for you in eliminating those response delays. How seriously have you considered changing your current system? For example, is it something you plan on in the future?"

SUSAN: "At some point we will have to make a change. The expense of a new system is probably holding us back right now more than anything else."

CINDY: "I understand. We have recently introduced a new finance plan that stores like yours can take advantage of. Basically, it offers no initial capital and the terms can be generous. Is that something you might be interested in?"

SUSAN: "No initial capital outlay may be very interesting to us. Is it a third-party finance situation?"

Cindy explains the finance plan details and Susan seems very interested. It's easy to see where this telemarketing call is headed. Cindy has identified a major objection, the money, and may have overcome it. She decides to further qualify.

CINDY: "It seems the primary reason for your not considering a new system is money. If that's the case, do you think our finance plan might resolve that issue?"

SUSAN: "To a certain extent I think it might. It would certainly make it easier for us to purchase."

CINDY: "Yes, it would. Susan, what I would like to do is set an appointment with you to discuss the needs of your store and also to talk with you about my organization and the services we offer. Next Tuesday is a good day for me; how does your schedule look?"

COMBINING THE SKILLS (continued)

Cindy got the appointment and then she asked further qualifying questions.

CINDY: "As the controller of the store would you make the decision to purchase a new system?"

SUSAN: "My job would be to look at the finances and prepare an analysis and recommendation."

CINDY: "Who would receive your recommendation?"

SUSAN: "Paul Sanders is our president, so I would discuss it with him. I think he might take it to the Board for approval. Of course, our floor managers would have a lot of input as well."

Cindy was satisfied with her telemarketing effort and the appointment. Cindy took a moment to jot down notes on her call with Susan and the information she had gained. Here's a quick summary of what she learned:

1. The store has an old system and a response time problem.

2. Money appears to be the key objection to a new system.

3. Susan is very interested in the finance plan.

4. Susan was interested in what Dale had done.

5. Susan is an important part of the decision-making process.

6. A positive recommendation from Susan is a must.

7. Paul Sanders will approve any decision. The Board of Directors may be involved.

8. The floor managers have major influence on the decision.

Would you say this was a well-qualified appointment; if so, why? _____

_____

_____

How many techniques can you identify in Cindy's call? _____

_____

_____

SUMMARY

Qualified appointments are obtainable whether you get them yourself or are fortunate enough to have a support employee making them for you. It's a matter of asking the prospective customer the right questions. Usually questions center around decision making, money, timing, procedures, future plans, problems, customer objectives, level of interest, needs, and a host of other factors.

When the prospect can't be qualified, it's okay to quit trying and move on. There is no point in forcing an appointment when the probability of selling your product or service is low.

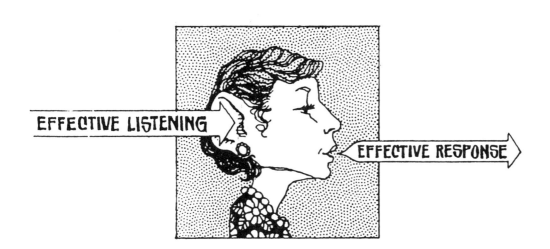

OPPORTUNITY #2: Offering Add Ons and Upgrades

An *add on* is the process of adding to the customer's order, often with ancillary products or service but also with other products that have customer appeal—specials, discounts, and so on. An *upgrade* is the process of moving the customer's buying decision to a higher quality and more costly product or service. The pet carrier mentioned earlier is an example of a telemarketer offering an upgrade.

The following is an illustration of a successful add-on program.

Tyler Stationery and Business Forms

The customer service operation at Tyler managed 80 percent of all orders over the telephone. The additional 20 percent were received by mail or fax. Large volumes of catalogs were printed and distributed. Customers shopped via the catalog, and then called customer service to place orders. Tyler realized the potential for upgrading or adding on to orders. Over time they integrated two telemarketing programs into their customer ordering process. Each program was designed to increase the gross amount of the average order.

Offering Specials

Tyler's first effort was to promote their "specials" with nearly every incoming call. The basic plan called for different "specials" to be offered for each six-week period. The six-week time frame was selected because a high percentage of customers placed orders with that frequency. The "specials" were price discounts, new products, two-for-one products, other promotions, and sale items.

Each customer service rep participated in training where specials were discussed, with a format presented of how and when to bring one to the attention of the customer. The reps participated in role play as a method of preparing themselves. The highlights of the telemarketing plan were as follows:

1. Reps were not required to mention "specials" unless they felt it was appropriate (see the next section for how to judge this) and fit with the customer conversation.

2. Reps were expected to discuss "specials" with at least 60 percent of all customers.

3. Only one "special" would be mentioned, per conversation, unless the customer asked about others.

4. The reps were asked to try and use particular statements/questions associated with each special. The statement/question was to be asked as the customer finished ordering unless it was otherwise appropriate. The three choices of questions were:

   a. "By the way, we are having a two-for-one sale on 9 x 12" white or manila envelopes. Do you use that size" [Next step: Explain the special.]

   b. "Are you aware of the special we have on rubber stamps?" [If customer is interested, explain special. If "no," abandon.]

   c. "Before we finish I should mention we are now offering three different brands of copier paper. Would you like to hear about them?" [If answer is "yes" continue, if "no," abandon.]

5. The reps were not required to try and sell the customer. If the customer expressed little or no interest, the subject was immediately dropped. The approach was defined as less than *soft sell*—it was called *soft service.*

Sales of the three products immediately increased as the reps encountered few problems in getting customers to consider the specials. In time the reps managed as many as six different specials during each six-week period. A few customers now ask, "Tell me about your specials."

BRAINSTORMING POTENTIAL ADD ONS

In many organizations offering an add on is just a natural part of the business. Buy a pair of new shoes, and the saleperson offers shoe polish. Buy a new tie and the salesperson suggests a new suit to go with it. Buy a car, there's the extended warranty. A new television brings about the offer of a service contract. Add ons are an important part of everyday business and sales.

The customer service reps at Tyler, in a training environment, brainstormed and came up with an add on for nearly every product they carried. A fraction of the add-on list looked like this:

(Product)	(Add Ons)
stapler	staples
ink pen	ink cartridges
pencils	leather pencil holder
rolodex	file cards
labels	label dispenser
calculator	batteries

The telemarketing plan called for an add on suggestion, if applicable, with every order. As before, the customer placed his or her order before the suggestion of an add on was delivered. The approach the reps used was brief and to the point. If the customer said "no," the add-on effort was quickly abandoned.

The reps learned to phrase questions and make statements in order to promote the add ons. A sampling of the statements made, and questions asked follows:

"Let's see, that's three new staplers. Shall I add a dozen boxes of staples?"

"Your order will go out this afternoon. Will you need index tabs for those file folders you ordered? We have both clear and colored."

"One carton of sealing tape. Do you need a new tape dispenser?"

This add on program worked. Order volume increased immediately. As part of the control process at Tyler, the customer service reps were periodically monitored during their telephone conversations to make certain add ons and specials were being mentioned. In nearly every meeting or training session now, add ons and specials are discussed and reinforced. Each rep is responsible for product knowledge of all specials and new add ons are brought to everyone's attention.

EXERCISE: *Identify Add Ons*

1. Does your organization have add ons for your service or product line? _____

   _____

2. Do you wait for the customer to ask before presenting add ons? _____

   _____

3. Is this the best course of action? _____

   _____

4. Could sales be improved if you suggested add ons on most customer calls?_____

   _____

Offering Upgrades: A Word of Caution

A quick way to irritate customers is to try—unprofessionally, and without skill—to add to their order or attempt to sell something new every time they call. When the effort is poorly executed it's an insult, not a telemarketing application. Asking order processors, clerks, service personnel and other nonsales personnel to upgrade routine orders without some form of training usually doesn't work and is unfair to the employee.

Despite the risks, telemarketing programs designed to upgrade and/or add to orders do work and can be successful.

Most organizations do not have professional sales people answering the telephone to take routine orders. Typically they are order processors or service employees with limited or no sales ability or experience. This adds to the dilemma of answering the question, "Will an upgrade program work for my organization?" In most organizations, the answer is "yes." However, the program must be well planned and executed.

BRAINSTORMING POTENTIAL ADD ONS (continued)

EXERCISE: Upgrading the Order

1. Identify a product you currently offer that can be upgraded.

   _____

2. Identify three specific benefits to the customer the upgrade offers.

   _____

   _____

   _____

3. Write out a brief script that you could use with customers to let them know about the product alternative and how they would benefit.

   _____

   _____

   _____

SUMMARY

Several factors stand out about the Tyler telemarketing program. The simplicity of the program is striking. Planning steps were used, and emphasis was placed on training. There was no attempt to convert the service reps into salespeople. The two telemarketing programs were controlled and monitored.

Very little was left to chance. The reps have latitude but only within prescribed parameters. The program is a success in large part because of these factors.

If upgrading and adding to orders has an application in your organization, the potential for increased sales is excellent.

OPPORTUNITY #3: Using After Service/Sale Telemarketing

Another basic, but effective telemarketing program is the after-sale or service call. Your organization completes a shipment or installation, resolves a major problem, or provides service of another kind. As part of an ongoing quality service program many organizations follow the service rendered with a telephone call inquiring about the customer's satisfaction level. For example:

TELEMARKETER: (following introductions) "The purpose of my call is to thank you for your order and to make certain you are satisfied with our service. If I may ask, how satisfied are you with our service?" [or] "Were you satisfied with the installation?"

Adding a Brief Survey to the Call

The basic idea of after-sales or service telemarketing is to test the customer's level of satisfaction by making a short to-the-point telephone call, and many organizations find it an opportune time to ask survey-type questions. This school of thought suggests that, with the customer already on the telephone and the conversation established, why not gather needed customer information? Some examples follow:

TELEMARKETER: "We are pleased that you are satisfied with everything. If you have a moment, would you mind answering three short questions about your perception of our advertising? It's part of a survey we are conducting."

TELEMARKETER: "On another issue, we are asking some of our customers about new products on the market. Since we value your opinion , I would like to ask you three or four questions. Would that be all right?"

TELEMARKETER: "We are conducting a survey, asking our customers to rank our services. If you have a moment, I would certainly appreciate hearing your opinions. May I ask two or three questions?"

OPPORTUNITY #4: Conducting Surveys

Learning what customers think and feel about your services and products is always valuable. In the discussion of customer surveys, a certain uniformity of questions and responses must be managed by the telemarketer in order to ensure the validity of the survey results.

How to Ask Questions

Let's take a moment and consider the kind of questions to ask. Generally closed-ended questions (answerable with a "yes" or "no") are used if you want a short answer. Open ended questions (how? why? what?) are used if you want more explanation. This is basic knowledge, but it's important to keep in mind when framing questions. Accuracy in a survey depends on identical questions being asked. The feedback, as well, needs to be recorded in a like manner.

Suppose your organization has decided to make follow-up calls to customers the day after a seminar is conducted at your site. Ideally, you want to know if the customers found the seminar worthwhile, if they are interested in the products and services presented, if they plan to purchase any of these products or services, and if they would like to attend future seminars. It sounds like a lot of information to get from one short conversation. The customer will have to stay on the telephone for a few minutes while each question is asked. Perhaps the inquiry can be reduced to seeking the most important information from the customer.

EXERCISE: Expanding Customer Responses

Think about it for a moment, and then write the most important questions you could ask of the seminar customer. Consider related and follow-up questions following the first primary question.

1. _____

2. _____

3. _____

4. _____

Now imagine a customer responding to your questions. Would certain responses lead to the need for other questions? For instance, suppose the customer was asked, "How worthwhile was the seminar for you?" If the customer replies, "It was very worthwhile," you will probably want to know what the customer liked about the seminar. If the customer says she didn't find the seminar worthwhile, you will want to know what she didn't like. With each question asked there is usually an important related question. It's not enough to know the customer is not planning on using your services. You must understand why. It's only part of the story to know that the customer thoroughly enjoyed the seminar. You must find out what they liked and why. These related questions need to be thought about in advance and phrased for the telemarketer. Why? Because you want the conversation to go smoothly and for all telemarketers to ask the identical questions in the same manner.

Here's an example of what happens when the telemarketer is armed only with the primary questions and is left on his own for related questions:

TELEMARKETER #1: "Please tell me what you liked most about the seminar and what you liked least."

CUSTOMER: "I was interested in the new widgets. The only negative about the seminar was it was too long."

Now the telemarketer has several possible related questions based on this response. He might ask any one of the following appropriate questions.

"What did you like about the new widgets?"

"Would you like more information on the new widgets?"

"How interested are you in purchasing the widgets?"

"How long do you think the seminar should have been?"

"What do you think could have been eliminated from the seminar?"

OPPORTUNITY #4 (continued)

Each of these questions has value, but the customer is not going to spend the time required for all these and other questions to be asked. Therefore, we have to make choices as to which questions are most important. Before deciding on the most important questions, let's see what questions telemarketer #2 poses. First she asks the same question. Let's assume the customer provides the same answer.

TELEMARKETER #2: "Please tell me what you liked most about the seminar and what you liked least?"

CUSTOMER: "I was interested in the new widgets. The only negative about the seminar was it was too long."

Telemarketer #2 has been instructed also to ask related questions, but since they are not preplanned she begins by asking a different question than telemarketer #1 did.

TELEMARKETER #2: "Were you impressed with the multimedia presentation?"

Let's suppose there are several employees following up on service calls. The result is four people asking different questions, thereby reducing the value of the customer input and creating confusion.

Composing Related Questions

Examine the primary questions you wanted to ask the customer. Which questions are the most important? Can they be phrased in a different manner that might eliminate the need for a related question? Does a related question need to be framed? Or can the related question be incorporated somehow into the primary question? Keep these questions in mind as you think about what you want to ask. Try the prior exercise again and write out one or two questions and include a related question if necessary. Be sure to ask questions that will provide the most important information.

EXERCISE: *Now Try Again*

1. Primary question: _____

   Related question: _____

2. Primary question: _____

   Related question: _____

REVIEW

There are several possible questions that might be asked. Since the primary purpose of the seminar was to promote the widgets, then the questions should be directed to that subject. Here is one way the conversation might flow:

> *"What did you think of our new widgets?"*

If the customer says he liked the product, the next question is:

> *"Will you be able to use these products in your business?"*

If the answer is "yes," then the conversation is moved to a discussion about when sales should contact the customer and so on. If the customer has a negative response to question #1, the telemarketer should try to determine what the objection to the product is. Once the objection is stated, the telemarketer—if skilled enough—might try and overcome the objection or just record the information and pass it on to sales.

We started with what appeared to be a need for many questions and reduced it to the most important questions along with related questions. From this point the conversation is tied to the customer's response and the telemarketer's desire to determine the customer's level of interest. To ensure that all telemarketers use the best questions, we may have to create a telemarketing script. Scripts are discussed later in this book.

A WORD ABOUT SURVEYS

Accuracy Is the Key

The key measurement of a telemarketing survey is accuracy and usefulness of the information. To ensure accuracy, uniformity of questions and responses must be managed well by the telemarketer. If the information gathered is questionable or believed to be inaccurate, then it is worthless. This applies whether it is your employees, a contractor, or a market research organization doing the telemarketing. If you have the slightest doubt in their ability, don't engage their services. The basic principle is the more skilled and professional the telemarketers, the more accurate and useful the information.

SUMMARY

Formal and lengthy customer telephone surveys require considerable skill on the part of the telemarketer. A script of questions and related questions is usually required in order to ensure uniform results from multiple telemarketers. Smaller information gathering programs generally require less skill and can be extremely worthwhile. When the customer is already on the inbound or outbound telephone call, it may be a good time to ask for a few quick opinions or perspectives on your services or products.

OPPORTUNITY #5: Collecting Overdue Accounts

Collecting overdue accounts has long been a strong telemarketing application. Up to thirty percent of the average organization's accounts will fall into the overdue category. Collecting these overdue accounts is not only an important function but a definite skill.

Successful organizations have a specific collection plan and at some point the overdue customer is called. Many organizations send a late notice letter first, then follow with a second late notice. Finally, a telephone call is made. Other organizations immediately call and avoid the late notice letter. Collections can usually be better controlled if calls are made to the overdue customer shortly after the bill or invoice becomes late.

Regardless of the system or procedure employed, there are important guidelines and legal requirements to follow regarding the collection calls.

NOTE: There are laws affecting debt collection that are beyond the scope of this book. For further information on legal requirements of the "Fair Debt Collection Practices Act" of 1977 and amended in 1986, contact the American Collectors Association in Minneapolis, Minnesota.

OPPORTUNITY #5 (continued)

Four Guidelines

1. Keep in mind you are collecting from and speaking with a customer who has done business with your organization in the past, and may in the future. Treat this customer with respect while firmly pursuing the collection.

2. Be prepared to address and respond to problems related to service, product, or personnel. The customer may not have made the payment because of such problems. Although the failure to pay the bill is not justified in the collector's view, it may be in the customer's.

3. Make certain you are prepared with current billing information. If there is any doubt regarding payment, don't call the customer. It doesn't make sense to expect the customer to straighten out your records. Get the facts organized first. Being familiar with the customer's payment record is important. Customers who have a long history of on-time payments may have problems with a collection call when the invoice is only a few days old. Customers can easily become irate when confronted with what is, in their view, an "oversight" or a "small matter." Good judgment is definitely required.

4. Try to help the customer when possible. Helping the customer may mean flexibility.

   • Offer a payment plan if needed.

   • Extend terms to an important customer (they tend to remember this generosity).

   • Allow the customer to participate in arranging a payment plan. (They more closely meet a payment if they help devise it.)

TELEPHONE SKILLS

Many of the telemarketing skills already discussed apply to collecting over-due accounts. The critical step of planning the call is a must. Knowing what is going to be said and when it is appropriate is a requirement for a successful collection call.

Equally important is anticipating the customer's objections, statements, excuses, or other reasons for being slow paying or not paying.

The structure of the typical collection call is as follows:

> ## *The Seven-Step Plan*
>
> **1.** Identify yourself and organization
>
> **2.** State the purpose of the call (*be direct and specific in your statements*)
>
> **3.** Clearly define the bills, invoices in question (*have the facts, including amounts and dates organized*)
>
> **4.** Gain customer concurrence that payment hasn't been made
>
> **5.** Develop a payment plan when needed (*allow for customer input*)
>
> **6.** Thank the customer for the cooperation
>
> **7.** Establish a plan for follow up

Using the seven-step plan, let's look at an example of successfully approaching the overdue customer. The technique demonstrated will apply to a wide variety of collection-type telemarketing calls.

TELEPHONE SKILLS (continued)

REACHING AN ACCEPTABLE ANSWER

COLLECTOR: Hi Jane. This is Sean Davis with the Rainbow Linen Supply Company. How are you today?

JANE: Good. What can I do for you?

COLLECTOR: I'm calling regarding our June 6th invoice. According to my records, it hasn't been paid and is currently six days late. Would you like the invoice number?

JANE: Sure.

COLLECTOR: It's 73709.

JANE: Let's see . . . we will issue a check on Friday the 14th.

COLLECTOR: Jane, in the past the hospital was always on time with our payments. What's causing this delay?

JANE: I'm not sure. Everything is getting backed up. The computer schedules the payments and I can't do much about it.

COLLECTOR: Do you think it would be beneficial for me to talk with the accounts payable manager about this situation?

JANE: Pam may be able to help you. (call is transferred)

COLLECTOR: Pam, my first concern is perhaps we are doing something wrong in how we submit our invoices. Is there something we can do differently that will help you meet the invoice due dates?

PAM: No. That's not a problem. I didn't think we were paying late very often. I knew we had a few delays earlier in the year, but since then I thought everything was okay.

COLLECTOR: In the last four months we have submitted thirteen invoices. Five were paid on time but six were late by at least seven days, and in one case it was twenty days overdue. One is still pending payment and Jane told me it was going to be late by about ten days.

PAM: I wasn't aware of this. Do you have the invoice numbers? I want to check this out.

COLLECTOR: When will you be able to give me some feedback?

PAM: I'll look into it right away. Our objective is to pay these invoices on time and it doesn't sound like we have done a very good job of it. I'll call you back this afternoon.

The collector managed this collection call well. He pursued the call until an acceptable answer was received. There were three times during the call when the average collector may have quit. They were:

(1) when the check issuance date was determined

(2) when Jane said she couldn't do much about the situation

(3) when the manager said she would look into the situation.

In regard to number three, the collector continued and was able to get a commitment for a callback.

Recurring Problem

Far too often collection call attempts end too soon. Small business, single proprietorships and others anxious to get payment are frequently so happy to learn when they are going to be paid that no attempt is made to expedite a late payment. They accept what is being said and feel there is nothing else they can do. Keep in mind that most large organizations have account payable objectives they are trying to reach. In this case the manager said to the collector, "It's our objective to pay these invoices on time." These organizations plan to pay their bills on time. Sometimes they need a collector to point out that delays exist. Here, the accounts payable manager didn't know about the late payments. As this example showed, it can be worthwhile discussing your late payment problems with someone with more authority.

TELEPHONE SKILLS (continued)

CASE STUDY: DFI

Using the seven-step plan, work through this case study. Suppose you were charged with the responsibility of collecting an overdue account. The DFI organization owes your company $5,000. The amount is forty-five days overdue. The accounting manager at DFI, Dave Edwards, says they were satisfied with your service and will pay the bill shortly. It has been ten days since anyone from your office spoke with Dave Edwards. You decide to call him. What are you going to say? Are there options you will offer Mr. Edwards? Keep in mind that DFI is an important account for your company. Take a moment and write out the key points of what you plan to say to Mr. Edwards.

_____

_____

_____

_____

_____

_____

_____

_____

_____

SUMMARY

Preparation for the collection call is important. Dates and amounts must be readily available along with notes or good memory to recall previous conversations. The opening seconds or moments of the collection call are very important. During this time the collector needs to convey the seriousness of the call to the customer. The seven-step call plan can be used to plan and think through collection calls before they are made. Despite the lack of payment, it's critical to keep in mind you are speaking with a customer. A customer who probably has done business with your organization in the past and will do so again in the future. Collecting overdue accounts, as experienced collectors know, is often a matter of persistence. Not giving up, and continuing the collection effort usually pays off.

OPPORTUNITY #6: Reactivating Inactive Accounts

In most organizations there are three types of customers. The ones you do business with, those you are still trying to capture, and those you used to do business with. A telemarketing opportunity exists with former customers. That is, reactivating inactive accounts.

One of the keys to success with this type of telemarketing is the completeness of your customer base information. For example:

- Do you know who to contact?

- Do you know their past buying history?

- What products did they purchase?

- How often and when?

The more information you have, the easer it will be to organize and implement a successful telemarketing program.

How to Approach Inactive Accounts

One school of thought is to approach these customers with questions like "We haven't heard from you in a while. Did we do something wrong? Was there a problem?" This method assumes there was a problem, and this is not necessarily correct. Yes, some leave because of poor service and other problems and these situations may have to be addressed before the account comes back. But also needs change, new personnel take over, competitors capture your accounts, customers move, and a variety of other reasons influence where customers do business.

The suggestion here is that inactive accounts be approached like a new account. Past problems—unless a major issue—need not be revisited. If previous problems are still on the customer's mind, she will mention them. Approach the customer with the benefits of doing business with you and, when possible, offer an added incentive. At the Tyler organization such an approach might sound like this:

> *"Mr. James, this is Brian Worth from Tyler Stationery and Business Forms. How are you today? The purpose of my call is to discuss a special we are having. In the past you have ordered several cartons of white bond paper from us and we currently have that same paper on sale at 20 percent off. That's quite a savings. Does that sound interesting to you?"*

OPPORTUNITY #6 (continued)

The difference here, between an old customer and a new one, is that the telemarketer knows the products the customer used to buy, and for the purposes of the call a special 20 percent discount was created. What if the customer isn't interested in the special? Does the customer then revert back to inactive status? No. Not yet anyway.

If the customer's response is "no," Brian's response is:

> *"Much of our inventory is on special at the moment. Are there other stationery or business form products you might be interested in at this time?"*

If the customer says "no" again, Brian's next response is:

> *"Mr. James, do you have a copy of our latest catalog?"*

If the answer is "no," Brian says he will send one. If the answer is "yes," Brian says:

> *"Good. I hope that you will be able to use the catalog and take advantage of the savings we're currently offering."*

If the customer fails to place an order, Brian tries to determine why he is no longer doing business with Tyler. Brian asks:

> *"Mr. James, it's been some time since we heard from you. If you don't mind my asking, is there a particular reason?"*

Regardless of the words and phrases the telemarketer uses, the intent is to get the customer interested in purchasing products or services. Far too often this type of program is a one-shot attempt at recapturing a customer. The customer is called and, if he doesn't respond immediately, no further attempts are made to interest him. A plan designed to recapture important customers starts with a telephone call offering a special. Next a mailer is sent, and then another telephone call. All during this attempt the program is monitored and managed. A simple flow chart of such a program is shown on page 83.

Plan for Recapturing an Inactive Account

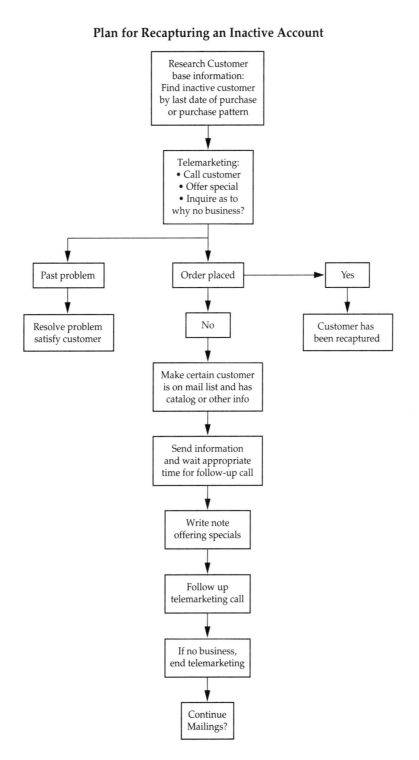

OPPORTUNITY #6 (continued)

EXERCISE: Recapturing Former Customers

1. How many former customers can you identify? _____

    _____

2. Are the numbers sufficient to think about a telemarketing program to
    recapture these customers? _____

    _____

SUMMARY

Attempts at recapturing customers are usually worthwhile. A telemarketing
call may be the key factor in such an attempt. The plan need not be complex. A straightforward customer call followed by mailers or other promotional material may do it. The one-shot approach usually doesn't work.
Multiple attempts and different approaches dramatically increase the probability of regaining a former customer.

OPPORTUNITY #7: Building Mail Lists

Telemarketing is a natural fit for establishing customer mail lists. Of course, the smaller the list the more manageable the telemarketing. Suppose you want to send a brochure or mailer to 1,000 potential customers. You have a list of the organizations and you know the job title of the person you want to receive your information, but don't know her name. Your objective is to be able to place a name with the job title for each organization on the mail list. Realistically, maybe 950 or 900 might be attainable.

Implementation

Let's assume for our example two temporary workers are hired to call and match a name to a job title. You estimate each temporary worker can complete 50 calls every day. Therefore, it will take 10 days to complete the calling. The temporary workers participate in limited training. Next, the calling begins.

TELEMARKETER: (speaking with whomever answers the telephone) ''Good morning. This is Jackie Clark with Slidefast. We have some important literature to send to your facility manager. May I have his or her name?''

If a name is given, take note. If refused, ask for the facility manager's office and repeat the opening remarks. Once the name is provided it's usually a good time to verify the address:

TELEMARKETER: (once the name has been provided) ''I show an address of 2378 T Street. Is that a valid address for Jan Stewart?''

Sounds simple, doesn't it? It is. It's a matter of professionally asking for the name and the ability to continue making call after call.

VALUE

Using telemarketing in order to confirm or obtain prospective customer names can greatly aid the results of a direct-mail program because, as you know, getting the information to the right party makes a major difference.

Let's quickly look at the costs associated with this telemarketing effort. The costs are two temporary employees at $11 per hour (salaries may be less in your area), including agency fee, times 160 hours (two weeks), which equals $1,760. Add $100 for long distance and the total becomes $1,860. Obviously, using existing clerical or other personnel may prove to be more cost effective.

Depending on the expected return, the costs will either be justified or not. The value of an accurate prospective customer list is very high when promoting most services or products. In the preceding example, if 950 names were gathered at a cost of $1,860, the cost per name is $1.95. Sound high? It depends on the return.

CASE STUDY: Selling the Training

In finding clients for customer service training, Cypress Consulting targeted thirty organizations where there seemed to be a match between the client's needs and the training expertise offered. Each organization was called by a clerical employee and was asked for the name of the customer service or technical support manager. Next a letter and brochure were sent to that individual. Four days were allowed for mail delivery and then the individual was called. The call went as follows:

"Good Morning. My name is Shannon Park. I recently sent you a brochure regarding a customer service training program we offer. Did you get a chance to read the material?"

RESULTS

Out of every thirty calls, at least one new client was always captured, and 20 percent of the time two or more were obtained. The training program offered was priced at several thousand dollars, so the results were satisfying. Success is greatly aided by sending the mail to the right person and then following with a telephone call.

OPPORTUNITY #8: Managing Business Reply Cards

In many organizations the difficulty is not generating the sales lead, but rather managing it once it is received. Planning a lead-response telemarketing program is an excellent way to follow up a trade show or publication advertising program. People fill out response cards for a variety of reasons. They:

- want more information

- want to collect your flyers and brochures

- may be interested in your services in the future

- might be ready to do business with you

The latter are the reply cards that deserve immediate attention. But first you must find those "right" cards, and usually that means contacting all the others.

Aging of response cards is often a problem. It is not uncommon for an organization to have a stack of leads that are many weeks old. As the lead ages, the customer's situation and interest changes, and her memory of your organization may fade as well. Potential customers are not impressed when they receive a call several weeks after a response card has been filled out. One way to avoid this problem is to plan a response to the leads in advance. As the leads arrive, respond. The following example provides some insight into how a basic "lead" telemarketing program might work.

EXAMPLE: *The Britton Group Attends a Trade Show*

The Britton organization assists individuals and corporations in finding overseas companies who will manufacture or assemble products. Britton participated in a small manufacturers trade show. They asked people who visited their booth to fill out a card if they wanted to be contacted by a representative to learn more about offshore manufacturing. They also advertised in trade-show literature that was sent to nearly every manufacturer in the country. The readers were asked to fill out a business response card if they were interested in a particular advertiser. The prospect stated on the card what they manufactured.

Within three weeks Britton had over 1,200 responses as a result of the trade-show booth and the advertising. They were surprised by the high number of leads generated. With a small staff, they weren't sure how to respond to the leads. They considered mailing brochures and other information to each lead but overruled that approach because of cost. Finally, it was decided to call and qualify each lead. A telemarketing program was planned to contact all 1,200 leads.

OPPORTUNITY #8 (continued)

Let's look at some of Britton's thinking and planning. They knew from experience that the majority of prospects were just looking for brochures and other file-cabinet information, and had no intention of actively pursuing offshore manufacturing. Others might have a future interest in offshore manufacturing but are not ready to seriously discuss the issue.

Britton decided on a telemarketing objective to qualify the top 50 prospects, who were qualified because of their available capital, product fit, and need, from the lead list of 1,200.

Following each telemarketing call, they wanted the prospect to be placed in one of four categories:

1. **Qualified:** Needs immediate sales follow up

2. **Not qualified at this time:** Future potential, add to mail list and send brochures

3. **Not qualified:** No further contact required

4. **Abandoned:** Unable to reach, did not return phone calls

EXERCISE: *Qualifying Prospects*

With the other planning steps completed, it was time to start the calling. Let's suppose you agreed to help make the telemarketing calls. In the space below jot down a few ideas on what you would say to the prospective customers and how you would qualify them. Keep the qualification steps we discussed earlier in mind. One suggestion: list the questions you would like answered from each prospect.

_____

_____

_____

_____

The following is how the telemarketer from Britton decided to handle the call.

TELEMARKETER: "Good afternoon, Mr. Keller. My name is Jan Walsh from Britton Offshore Manufacturing. I'm calling to thank you for expressing interest in our company. You filled out a response card in conjunction with the Small Manufacturers Trade Show. Do you recall?"

KELLER: "Yes, I do remember. I stopped at your booth. Your display was quite interesting."

Jan opened up this conversation quite well. She has positioned the call as a response to the card by beginning with a "thanks for your interest introduction." Basically, she acts as if she is returning the customer's call. This approach certainly takes the "cold" out of the call and paves the way for the qualifying questions.

TELEMARKETER: "The response card you completed said you were interested in learning more about our organization. Are you considering offshore manufacturing?"

There are numerous questions that might be asked, but Jan cut right to the heart of the matter with her direct but very appropriate question.

KELLER: "Yes. We are thinking about it."

TELEMARKETER: "If you should move offshore, would this be an expansion or would you be replacing your existing domestic manufacturing operations?"

OPPORTUNITY #8 (continued)

Jan learns Mr. Keller's organization will be expanding. She next asks questions about the timing of the expansion and learns it is in the near future. She familiarizes Mr. Keller with the capabilities of Britton and he asks several questions. Jan also learns Mr. Keller's company is *public*, so she knows the salesperson can look at their financial health before calling for an appointment. Jan places Mr. Keller in the qualified category. Would you do the same?

Questions

The following is a list of qualifying questions that might be used in this situation. Several of them, modified to your needs, should apply to your next response card telemarketing program.

- ▶ According to your response card, you manufacture tennis racquets. Do you manufacture other products?

- ▶ Which products would you consider taking offshore?

- ▶ When you consider offshore, do you think in terms of having your own facility or subcontracting the manufacturing?

- ▶ Have you budgeted for offshore manufacturing?

- ▶ If you should decide to move offshore, when do you think that might take place?

- ▶ I know that lower cost is one of your primary considerations in thinking about offshore; are there other considerations?

- ▶ How do you think we can best help you?

- ▶ Is the timing right for a meeting with one of our representatives?

- ▶ Shall I have a representative call and set up an appointment?

MEASURING THE PROGRAM

Lead generation programs are pretty easy to measure and track. First you have the expense of the lead. In the Britton case $6,000 was spent on the trade booth including personnel costs and transportation, and another $4,000 on advertising. So, for $10,000 Britton generated 1,200 leads. The cost per unit is $83.00. The majority of these leads are not qualified; in fact Britton felt they could handle only 50 well-qualified leads. The cost becomes $200.00 per unit. Add in the telemarketing expense and the cost per qualified lead increases again. Is it worth it?

Britton sells high-cost services. One new client might wipe away all expenses many times over. There is also the value of trade-show exposure and the good will created.

Tracking a program of this type may require a long period of time. If six months or a year down the line four new clients are suddenly captured, it's important to remember where they came from.

REVIEW

1. In your organization, are business leads generated? _____
   _____

2. If so, how do you respond to the prospective customer? _____
   _____

3. If you haven't been using telemarketing to respond, how well do you think it might work for you? _____
   _____

4. Use the planning steps we discussed earlier and build a telemarketing plan to respond to those important leads. _____
   _____

SUMMARY

Lead generation programs are worthwhile. Planning the response to the leads is critical and when telemarketing is used, the planning steps discussed earlier apply. Aging of leads is a serious problem. Timing is an important part of success and the prospect should be contacted soon after the response card is sent in. Qualifying prospects is a never-ending process. Part of that process is the willingness to abandon and disqualify prospects. As in other telemarketing programs, a measurement and tracking system needs to be established and followed.

SECTION

V

Telemarketing
in Action

CASE STUDY: A Company Does It Well

If you visited LifeScan Inc. in Milpitas, California, you would observe, first hand, the value of organized, well-planned telemarketing. LifeScan presents an outstanding example of customer service delivered over the telephone.

LifeScan makes ONE TOUCH® brand meters and test strips, and ancillary products used by health care professionals and diabetics to determine blood sugar levels, and hence, the effectiveness of prescribed medication, diet, and exercise programs.

Objective

LifeScan's customer service is driven by its mission statement: "We are committed to providing rapid, accurate, caring response and continued support to the blood glucose monitoring community: patients and health care professionals, LifeScan's distribution network and the LifeScan product team."

LifeScan realized that to better meet its objectives and to continue to increase sales—and thus market share—changes were needed. Adding to its concern was the growing sophistication of the LifeScan product line, which required even more expertise from its representatives.

LifeScan had already established high performance standards for their service reps and knew that the position would continue to require well-rounded individuals with knowledge about diabetes as well as telephone, communication, fact finding, and listening skills. In addition, they have to be versatile enough to talk with a health care professional on one call, and then a user of their meters on the next. In between, an authorized distributor might call and place an order. In short, the demand on these employees would continue to grow.

LIFESPAN'S SOLUTION

The solution for LifeSpan, following much study, was market segmentation. Rather than continue to demand more and more from its representatives—asking them to be all things to all customers—LifeScan established a market segmentation plan. Customer Services was divided into four distinct market segments, and the representatives became specialists within their own market segment.

The Market Test

LifeScan did not conduct a market test as such. However, in preparation for market segmentation the customer calling patterns from each market segment were extensively studied, in order to avoid staffing and other problems. From the beginning LifeScan set high standards for response time to customers. For example, the marketing support group established a service objective that all calls be answered within thirty seconds. The order services group, in responding to distributors, set an objective that all calls be answered within two rings.

The Plan

The four market segments LifeScan decided upon were Order Services, Health Care Professionals, End Users, and Marketing Support. Each segment is identified by an 800 number. An ACDS (automatic call distributing system) routes the calls to the correct representative. To gain a competitive advantage and provide even stronger service, the end-user line is available seven days a week, 24 hours a day.

MONITORING AND CONTROLLING

The ACDS provides considerable data on calls including customer wait times, call duration, the "live" status of each representative, and many other valuable measurements that are shared with the representatives on a daily basis.

Additional monitoring is an ongoing activity at LifeScan customer services. Supervisors and outside training personnel observe calls and recommend ways to enhance existing performance. All representatives, whether new or long-time, participate in the monitoring and feedback system.

Training

Training is important at LifeScan. Each newly hired customer service representative begins training with participation in a six-week training class. The topics covered include LifeScan products, diabetes, customer satisfaction, telephone skills, and data management. The classes are conducted by customer service trainers and subject matter experts. This six-week orientation is intensive, and considerable testing for understanding is required during the classes. Refresher and other subject matter training is ongoing at LifeScan.

Scripting

LifeScan employees are familiar enough with their jobs that mental scripting is automatic; formal or written scripts are used for some topics to make certain that important new facts are covered uniformly or to ensure legal correctness.

Operational Costs

Like other successful organizations LifeScan constantly reviews costs and looks for savings. By monitoring the type of call received, LifeScan has found ways to reduce the number of calls while maintaining quality service. For example, teams of employees are formed to find cost-effective ways to reduce the number of customer calls. In several situations the customer is given the option of calling or mailing in a form for routine reorders or orders for ancillary items.

MONITORING AND CONTROLLING
(continued)

Telephone Ordering

The order services department is open to all authorized LifeScan distributors to order products. Although there is not an "add to the order" telemarketing program as previously described, representatives do mention ancillary products to the distributors if there appears to be a need for a complete care system.

SUMMARY

LifeScan has created a highly successful customer services department that manages thousands of calls per month. Using the telemarketing planning steps discussed earlier, LifeScan has established a market segmentation plan—using telemarketing—that is driven by an unswerving commitment to providing the best possible customer service.

SECTION

VI

Scripting: A Telemarketing Essential

SCRIPTING YOUR MESSAGE

What a dreaded word "scripting" can be for both the telemarketer and prospect. As you sit down to dinner the telephone rings, you answer, and an entry-level telemarketer starts reading a script. The script includes questions, assumptions, and benefits all incorporated into a script that is read. If you ask a question or make a statement that is not in keeping with the script, the telemarketer often loses his place and confusion takes over. For you the call is annoying. For the telemarketer it means a very high volume of calls before a prospect listens to the complete script and agrees to purchase whatever is being offered. Once again, the telemarketer is dialing with the hope of eventually finding the connection.

Scripting Is Necessary

Scripting is fundamental and always included by successful telemarketers. Does this mean they always have a written script? No. However, they have at least a mental script of what they are going to say and when and how they are going to say it. Responses are prepared and delivered automatically as are questions and methods of attacking objections. To watch a salesperson on the telephone in complete command of everything he says—with an appropriate response every step of the way—is an excellent display of telemarketing. This type of telemarketer depends less on volume of calls and more on quality effort.

Controlling What Is Said

Controlling the telemarketing operation is a management function and that may include what is said to the prospect or customer. Earlier we discussed the importance, in many situations, of the telemarketers making similar statements and asking the same questions in order to ensure quality and uniformity. In this way the results will be accurate.

In a survey-type of program perhaps the script is only one or two questions. In other circumstances it will be lengthy, with standardized questions, statements, and responses. Whether the script is short, long, written, or mentally prepared it is always required.

SCRIPTING YOUR MESSAGE (continued)

Should You Read a Script?

The script serves as an outline—not something to be read. Reading a script is easily detected by the customer and is an automatic turnoff. Even the smoothest actor may have difficulty disguising the fact he is reading. Just watch your local news. Some reporters expertly manage the teleprompter while others struggle with it.

The Script Is the Message

The message the organization wants to convey is the script. It consists of statements, responses, questions, and—in sophisticated scripts—actions such as surprise, humor, enthusiasm, concern, and just about everything else a quality telemarketer is capable of conveying over the telephone. To better understand scripts, let's build one.

EXERCISE: Script Building

Congratulations! Your boss calls and asks you to build a script for the telemarketing center. She further explains the script will introduce the new 700-series widget. The telemarketing plan calls for all customers currently using the 500 series to be called and offered the upgraded 700 series. The benefits to the 700 series are larger capacity, smaller size, speed, and greater cost efficiency. Sales will call the larger accounts, and the telemarketing center will contact the rest. What are you going to script for the telemarketers? Write out two introductory statements. Be sure to include possible questions to get the customer involved.

Introductory Statements:

1. _____

   _____

   _____

2. _____

   _____

   _____

Once you have selected the best introductory remarks, step #1 of your telemarketing script is complete. All telemarketers will use your opening statements. Step #2 can vary but usually a key question is asked at this point, a question like, "Does that sound interesting?" or "How well have the 500-series widgets been working for you?" The point is to get the customer more involved and to direct the conversation into upgrading to the 700-series widgets. List three possible key questions that might follow the introductory remarks.

Key Questions:

1. _____

_____

2. _____

_____

3. _____

_____

Step #2 is complete. Step #3 is to consider the most likely customer responses from the questions in step #2 and then script a reply to each response. Some will argue this isn't necessary. Perhaps so—if you have skilled employees staffing the phones who can respond as needed! But, if you have a group with varying skill levels, the script will help maximize the sales opportunity. To see how well what has been scripted might play, let's look at a customer conversation. The introductory statements might look as follows:

TELEMARKETER: "Good afternoon, Mr. Sinclair, this is Debbie Martin from ACME Widget and Supply. If you have a moment I would like to briefly discuss with you a new widget product we are introducing. It's called the 700 series. Have you heard much about it?"

The standard customer reply might be as follows:

MR. SINCLAIR: "Yes. It was mentioned in the trade magazine last month but there wasn't much information."

SCRIPTING YOUR MESSAGE (continued)

Next, the telemarketer continues with the introductory statements and involves the customer by asking several questions:

TELEMARKETER: "Perhaps the best way to describe it is to contrast it with the 500 series. How many 500 series do you have working?"

MR. SINCLAIR: "We have six."

TELEMARKETER: "Are they at full capacity?"

MR. SINCLAIR: "Four are. We have had a lot of growth the last two years."

TELEMARKETER: "I see. When do you plan to bring the other two 500 series up to full capacity?"

MR. SINCLAIR: "Probably this summer. Early fall at the latest."

The telemarketer now presents the 700 series widget, stressing the capacity benefit.

TELEMARKETER: "To give you an example of the full potential of the new 700 series, you could replace six 500 series at full capacity with only four 700 series. In fact, in that situation the 700 series will still have approximately 20 percent growth capability."

NOW, ASK THE KEY QUESTION

Now, the key question:

> "Does that sound like something you would be interested in?"

The introductory remarks including several questions are complete, and the first key question was asked. Let's list the most likely replies to the key question. The customer might say:

> "Yes. I'm interested."

> "I might be. What does it cost?"

> "It depends. What are the costs?"

> "With that kind of capacity the widget must be considerably larger. I'm not sure we have the space."

Let's assume the telemarketer will hear one of these four responses from the majority of customers. Therefore, the script must address a reply to a customer who is interested or concerned about costs or space.

Scripting Review

Let's quickly review. The script contains introductory statements followed by a key question that produces a response that provides the first hint of the customer's level of interest. We now need to script the next response. Our script narrows the conversation until the customer's interest level is determined and then ends with some sort of action. The conclusion in our example might be the sale of a new 700 series widget, a promise to send product information, perhaps a referral to sales, a planned follow-up date, or just noting the customer isn't interested. This type of script takes on a flow chart look or can be laid out with actual statements and questions for the telemarketer to follow. An example of each is given on page 106.

SCRIPTING YOUR MESSAGE (continued)

Script Flow Chart Example

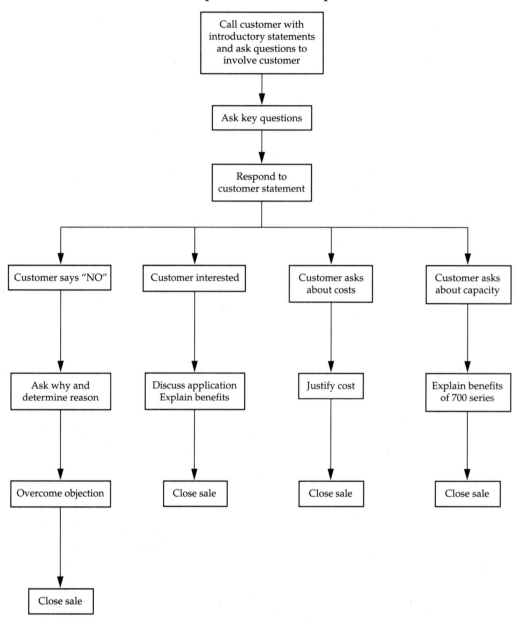

A Sample Script

Introductory Statement:

Good afternoon, Mr./Mrs. _____. I'm Sally from ACME Widget and Supply. If you have a moment I would like to briefly discuss with you a new widget we are introducing. It's called the 700 series. Have you heard much about it?

[If customer has seen the trade magazine article last month, use statement #1. If not, use statement #2.]

Statement #1:

That was an interesting article the magazine published. The 700 series is getting a lot of positive notice within the industry. Perhaps the best way to describe it is to contrast it with the 500 series. How many 500-series widgets do you presently have working?

Statement #2:

The 700 series is getting a lot of positive notice within the industry. Perhaps the best way to describe it is to contrast it with the 500 series. How many 500-series widgets do you presently have working?

[Customer will respond with number working.]

Question:

Are they at full capacity?

[Customer will respond with statement or discussion regarding capacity. Keep in mind the more capacity used, the greater the need for the 700 series. Next explain the benefits of the 700-series capacity using the conversion chart.]

Statement #3:

One 700-series widget can replace two 500 series at 70 percent capacity. In your case with _____ 500 series and an average capacity of _____ that means you could reduce the number of installed widgets by _____. To do that you need to order _____ 700 series widgets.

SCRIPTING YOUR MESSAGE (continued)

Key Question:

Does that sound like something you would be interest in?

[The customer will respond the majority of time with one of several responses.]

The script continues on and addresses each probable customer response. As in the flow chart example if the customer inquires about cost, capacity, or says she is or is not interested, the telemarketer has a standard scripted reply. The script is designed to move the conversation closer to a sale or other action.

EXERCISE: Scripting

1. Has this brief section changed your persective on scripting?

2. Are the sales or service people in your organization delivering the best possible message to your customers?

3. How much is left to chance?

SUMMARY

Scripts take on many forms. Mental scripting works for many, while others need an outline or actual worded script in front of them during the call. The script can serve as a basic guideline or as a management tool to help control what is said to customers or prospects and how products or services are presented. Sometimes there are legal considerations or product claims that must be closely monitored and scripts therefore become a necessity. Quality scripts can be created and are often approached by addressing the desired action; for instance, wanting the customer to buy a 700-series widget.

Well-intentioned scripts can easily be put aside by telemarketers. Sometimes it's positive because the written script has been mentally scripted. At other times it's a negative situation because employees have strayed from the script and the desired message or response is no longer being sent. If the telemarketers and management want an exact message delivered, one which will maximize the sales or other opportunity, they need to monitor the calls and insist upon following the script.

ADAPTING TELEMARKETING TO YOUR ORGANIZATION

We hope this book has helped change your perception of telemarketing, what it is, and what it may be able to do for your organization. Telemarketing has its place in the marketing mix but, like other ventures, it must be planned and executed with skill. The examples we looked at hopefully serve the purpose of informing you and provide ideas that may be applied to your situation.

The Future

Telemarketing will continue to grow and new and different applications will be uncovered. As customer telephone activity continues to increase, telemarketing and customer skills will blend together and become increasingly important. In the LifeScan Inc. example we saw such a blend. In that model, a near-perfect telemarketing application was well organized and executed.

Experts tell us that most of the future jobs in the United States will be found in the service sector. Jobs requiring telemarketing skills fall into this category. The demand for highly skilled telemarketers will continue to soar as organizations get more involved in telemarketing. The competitive edge can be gained through telemarketing. LifeScan, Inc. used a market segmentation application for their customer service department and stretched their telephone response to seven days a week, 24 hours a day in order to gain an edge on their competitors.

Finding the telemarketing application within your organization may provide a whole new stream of profits—and in many cases improve service to your customer base.

BIBLIOGRAPHY

"Achieving Success with Call Center Management." *Telemarketing*, August 1993.

"First a Solid Foundation." *Telemarketing*, June 1991.

Mondello, Candace L. *Credits and Collections*. California: Crisp Publications, 1991.

Shaw, Terry. "Dial A for Annoyance." *San Jose Mercury News*, 16, December 1991.

Stevens, Mark. "Collecting Lagging Bills Will Streamline Your Business." *San Jose Mercury News*, 21, May 1988.

OVER 150 BOOKS AND 35 VIDEOS AVAILABLE IN THE 50-MINUTE SERIES

We hope you enjoyed this book. If so, we have good news for you. This title is part of the best-selling *50-MINUTE™ Series* of books. All *Series* books are similar in size and identical in price. Many are supported with training videos.

To order *50-MINUTE* Books and Videos or request a free catalog, contact your local distributor or Crisp Publications, Inc., 1200 Hamilton Court, Menlo Park, CA 94025. Our toll-free number is (800) 442-7477.

50-Minute Series Books and Videos Subject Areas . . .

Management
Training
Human Resources
Customer Service and Sales Training
Communications
Small Business and Financial Planning
Creativity
Personal Development
Wellness
Adult Literacy and Learning
Career, Retirement and Life Planning

Other titles available from Crisp Publications in these categories

Crisp Computer Series
The Crisp Small Business & Entrepreneurship Series
Quick Read Series
Management
Personal Development
Retirement Planning